Dear Maggie:

Thank you for your help!

`D0961171`

Elvis

MEI XU

Founder of CHESAPEAKE BAY CANDLE

BURN

HOW GRIT,
INNOVATION,
AND A
DASH OF LUCK
IGNITED A
MULTI-MILLION DOLLAR
SUCCESS STORY

WILEY

Copyright © 2021 John Wiley & Sons. All rights reserved.

Published by John Wiley & Sons, Inc., Hoboken, New Jersey.

Published simultaneously in Canada.

No part of this publication may be reproduced, stored in a retrieval system, or transmitted in any form or by any means, electronic, mechanical, photocopying, recording, scanning, or otherwise, except as permitted under Section 107 or 108 of the 1976 United States Copyright Act, without either the prior written permission of the Publisher, or authorization through payment of the appropriate per-copy fee to the Copyright Clearance Center, Inc., 222 Rosewood Drive, Danvers, MA 01923, (978) 750-8400, fax (978) 646-8600, or on the Web at www.copyright.com. Requests to the Publisher for permission should be addressed to the Permissions Department, John Wiley & Sons, Inc., 111 River Street, Hoboken, NJ 07030, (201) 748-6011, fax (201) 748-6008, or online at http://www.wiley.com/go/permissions.

Limit of Liability/Disclaimer of Warranty: While the publisher and author have used their best efforts in preparing this book, they make no representations or warranties with respect to the accuracy or completeness of the contents of this book and specifically disclaim any implied warranties of merchantability or fitness for a particular purpose. No warranty may be created or extended by sales representatives or written sales materials. The advice and strategies contained herein may not be suitable for your situation. You should consult with a professional where appropriate. Neither the publisher nor author shall be liable for any loss of profit or any other commercial damages, including but not limited to special, incidental, consequential, or other damages.

For general information on our other products and services or for technical support, please contact our Customer Care Department within the United States at (800) 762-2974, outside the United States at (317) 572-3993 or fax (317) 572-4002.

Wiley publishes in a variety of print and electronic formats and by print-on-demand. Some material included with standard print versions of this book may not be included in e-books or in print-on-demand. If this book refers to media such as a CD or DVD that is not included in the version you purchased, you may download this material at http://booksupport.wiley.com. For more information about Wiley products, visit www.wiley.com.

Library of Congress Cataloging-in-Publication Data is Available:

ISBN 9781119695929 (Hardcover)
ISBN 9781119695943 (ePDF)
ISBN 9781119695899 (ePub)

Cover Design: Paul McCarthy
Cover Image: © Getty Images | EveMilla

SKY10024693_020421

I dedicate this book to my father, Jianxu Xu, and my mother, Yanyun Lin. Although we have been apart for such a long time, I brought their love, dedication, and work ethic with me as I traveled the world. This is as much their story as it is my own.

Contents

Prologue vii

1 A Tale of Two Chinas 1

2 American Odyssey 33

3 American Entrepreneurs 57

4 Fragrance Forward 93

5 Made in America 119

Conclusion 145

About the Author 149

Acknowledgments 153

Index 157

Prologue

When I first landed on American soil in 1991, I had little money and even less direction. Precisely 21 years later, in 2012, I sat next to President Barack Obama at a roundtable discussion with fellow CEOs, sharing my policy recommendations about American entrepreneurship and manufacturing.

During the intervening years, I created a company in America and built a factory there to manufacture its products, realizing my version of the American Dream. In this book, I describe how I did it. As I hope to convince you, the American Dream remains vital and accessible to all of us, so long as we're willing to *burn*—igniting that flame within and pursuing our passion with courage and creativity, innovating and adapting to our constantly changing society.

It took me a while to activate and stoke my own internal flames. Growing up, I'd trained in China to become a diplomat. After this career path became impossible, I secured a visa to the United States with dreams of becoming a journalist. The best job I could find after graduating with my master's degree was for a medical device company, performing low-end administrative work for $19,000 a year. I could only pivot to a new life of purpose when I followed the path of many immigrants to America. Mobilizing my experience, savvy, intuition, and professional skills, I became an entrepreneur, creating products that filled a specific market niche.

Like many immigrants, I succeeded in business by using my cross-cultural background to reimagine stale consumer categories and places, infusing them with new meaning and value. It took an immigrant like me to see Chesapeake Bay as a beacon of nature and peace rather than as ugly and polluted, as many of my friends and neighbors regarded it. This piece of real estate exercised such a hold on me that it became enmeshed in my personal and professional identities. It's the place I've called home since moving to the United States, and it's the region on which I took a huge financial gamble in opening a factory. Whether you're an entrepreneur, business leader, or simply interested in America's ongoing business strength, I hope you'll come away from this book appreciating the contributions of immigrants, and be inspired to look at landscapes, product categories, and social problems with new eyes.

I also hope you'll think a bit differently about innovation, that cornerstone of American prosperity. The word "innovation" usually conjures up groundbreaking technical breakthroughs. To create a diverse and robust economy, however, entrepreneurs must take a broader view of innovation, training their talents on "mundane" industries and product categories like exercise equipment, investment tools, Chino clothes, candles, and underwear. Read the following pages to discover how I stumbled into the candle industry, using my creativity to transform these once-boring products into fashion items that enhance and elevate a person's home and life. This book is my rousing call for more entrepreneurs to similarly push the boundaries of innovation, creating a set of products and services that solve consumer and environmental problems, making life more efficient and enjoyable in the process.

In many ways, my success with candles is unsurprising in today's market where creative leaders increasingly supplant business-savvy MBAs and technocrats in achieving market success and social impact.[1] I use the term "design leadership" to refer to today's creativity-driven economy. Design leaders are creative businesspeople who prioritize their service or product's core "design" or message above profitability, price, shareholder-value maximization, and the like. Instead of leveraging design to chase margins and profitability, design leaders use it to drive sales, marketing, manufacturing, and other business activities. We're long familiar with the world's legendary design leaders. Instead of competing on price, Steve Jobs harnessed the power of design-driven innovation when creating and manufacturing his world-changing Macintosh computer and iPhone line. Elon Musk accomplished the same, parting from fossil fuel–inspired profit models and design templates to fashion an automobile as intuitive to operate as an iPhone and heralding a new era in which clean energy replaces the environmentally damaging combustion engine.

Though I built Chesapeake Bay atop these same foundations of design leadership, letting innovation and creativity dictate business decisions, it was only by controlling manufacturing that I could maximize creativity and fuel my products' popularity among consumers. When factories in Asia refused to work with my design-driven collections, my passion and vision convinced my sister to quit her job and build a factory to help grow my business. Together, we created new consumer-product lines in the home fragrance and wellness industries and brought these luxuries, once reserved for wealthy department-store consumers, to a mainstream American market. But I could only achieve peak innovation when I stopped outsourcing manufacturing, breaking with my US counterparts in reshoring many of my operations to America.

By bringing industrial processes in-house, I increased the quality of my source ingredients, marrying manufacturing and innovation to reach my highest creative potential. In America, my company accomplished the seemingly impossible: building a factory outside Baltimore, where manufacturing was long considered dead. I hope other product categories follow my lead, leveraging design leadership and creative manufacturing to better observe and respond to markets, decrease costs, increase innovation, and improve quality.

As I told President Barack Obama during our meeting at the White House, I was confident that design-driven entrepreneurship and thoughtful manufacturing would power growth and prosperity throughout the global economy. But much has changed since then. During my entrepreneurial career, people and ideas traversed the globe, governments more freely cooperated in international accords, and technological innovation powered exciting new breakthroughs. Today, the world has become more pessimistic, protectionist, and insular. Instead of understanding technology and globalism as contributors to our collective prosperity, people have experienced their corrosive effects on democracy, economic abundance, and human happiness. But I still believe the words I told the president. As I hope to persuade you in the following pages, design leadership remains vital to a robust, global economy.

As a Chinese immigrant to America, I constantly encounter the dreaded America-versus-China question. Will America remain the global superpower, or will China take its place? I object to the question because I hope America and China both remain strong, resolving their differences and becoming good economic partners again. But the larger question of America's fate is deeply personal to me. America, I believe, will always be preeminent to the extent that my story remains possible. As long as a foreign national can arrive on its shores as an alien and then appear at the White House 20 years later, rest assured that America will remain the world's beacon of opportunity and prosperity.

—**Mei Xu**

Endnote

1. For this overview, I am indebted to Daniel H. Pink, *A Whole New Mind* (New York: Riverhead Books, 2005), 1–4. Pink's powerful and penetrating book helped inspire my ideas of design leadership.

1

A TALE OF TWO CHINAS

It's a balmy summer evening in the early 1970s, and a group of families from my town are seated in folding bamboo chairs or sprawled on blankets in an outdoor stadium. We're all watching a state-sponsored movie on a grainy, black-and-white film projector. Midway through China's Cultural Revolution, our country is sealed off from the outside world. No headline news stories, no discussion of "current events," and no popular culture from other countries filter into our consciousness. Visits from foreign dignitaries are rare. This outdoor movie, featuring what many would now label "propaganda," is our major form of popular entertainment. And here, on this massive screen, the outside world has made a brief and tantalizing appearance. The movie flashes scenes from the king of Cambodia, Norodom Sihanouk, and his princess consort, Queen Monique, paying a state visit to China.

A young child, probably only five or six years old, I stare up at the screen, transfixed by the film's charisma, glamour, and pageantry. The Cambodian king smiles amiably and extends his hands in the air, greeting throngs of Chinese citizens packed along either side of a grand boulevard in Beijing. He stands up in the backseat of a convertible with Chinese statesman Deng Xiaoping on his left and Queen Monique on his right, the latter wearing an elegant black dress with her hair loosely fastened. In the background, rectangular flags wave behind rows of youth in marching bands, heralding the visit with drums and wind instruments. Another image shows the royals walking on a red carpet, as children of my own age politely bow and offer them flowers. The projector also flashes a photograph of the king's 1941 coronation ceremony, when he wore a towering, bejeweled headpiece strapped tightly to his chin; a lavish, geometrically detailed chest piece; and a disinterested look on his face.

Historians will tell you that this visit proved inauspicious for the king's domestic ambitions. He was subsequently deposed and spent decades cozying up to foreign powers, eventually forging a tragic compact with Pol Pot and his brutal Khmer Rouge dictatorship. Had I been older, I might have noticed the vacant expression on his face during his coronation ceremony. This leader had little taste for forging geopolitical alliances and would rather have produced movies and hosted dinner parties. But I had no sense of such matters; I was simply taken by the exoticism of it all. This colorful spectacle of a state visit marked my first inkling that a different life existed beyond the confines of our dormitory apartment, neighborhood, and city.

A young Mei on the banks of Hangzhou's West Lake (ca. 1984).

A Peaceful Harbor

This is not to say that our world lacked appeal. I grew up in Hangzhou, long revered as one of China's most beautiful cities, and even considered a "paradise on earth."[1] When China embarked on industrialization in the 1950s, many of its cities adopted a Soviet architectural style and approach to urban planning that allowed industry to flourish. My hometown, by contrast, sought to become a socialist "Geneva of the East."[2] Capitalizing on the city's historic prominence as a place of tourism, scenic beauty, and religious pilgrimage, communist leaders spared it from an aggressive takeover and industrial overhaul, and instead prioritized aesthetic concerns and environmental purity. These leaders made strenuous efforts to protect the city's famed West Lake from pollution, cultivating healthy fish production and maintaining the area's temples, trees, and gardens.

Vestiges of Hangzhou's unique urban development path still exist today. While sleek office towers and futuristic engineering marvels dominate the skylines of megacities like Beijing and Shanghai, sometimes shrouding their historical treasures, my hometown's natural beauty casts an almost magical charm. The centerpiece of Hangzhou's scenic appeal—its beautiful West Lake, situated to the west of the old city—remains visible from most of the downtown high rises. You'll see the surface dotted with bamboo canoes or glimpse pedestrians strolling along one of the many famed stone bridges. In the springtime, blossoming peach trees, willows, and green tea trees imbue the city with a different type of magic, one almost redolent with spirituality. Buddhism long thrived in the area, and each spring pilgrims flocked to the city's temples and other religious centers dotting the lake district or surrounding countryside.[3]

Amidst this beauty, our family lived a relatively simple life. We occupied a standard-issue room in one of the many dormitory housing units that lined the city's north end. Mom and Dad shared a queen-size bed, while nearby my sister Li and I occupied a single twin. I'd slept there since the age of two after my parents added an additional plank to Li's bed, making it more spacious and comfortable for two little bodies. A desk stood on one side of the wall, along with two wooden stools, which could serve as a workstation. During mealtimes, when we moved the furniture to the center of the apartment, the desk doubled as a dining room table. We owned a wardrobe chest, an old-fashioned transistor radio, a few wooden trunks to store our winter gear, and two or three pairs of shoes each. We shared a public toilet (without a shower) and communal kitchen area with other families on our floor. Once a week, we ventured to a larger public bathroom to bathe. My parents constantly worked, leaving us free to climb trees and play with the neighborhood children. We had no reason to suspect that any area was dangerous or off-limits. Even if we sometimes yearned for more food, we were carefree and content, roaming the city as far and wide as our imaginations could take us.

Only in retrospect could one describe this existence as poor or even bland. I certainly didn't experience it this way. I was recently reminded of my childhood home when I dropped my son Alex off for his first year of college at the University of Chicago. All students occupy precisely half a dormitory room, their portion equipped with a small bed, spare desk, and wiring outlets, and they all share a big kitchen. There's no place to hide—if you have a fight with someone, everyone can hear it. Take away all the modern gadgets, and it isn't so different from conditions in my native Hangzhou. No one would call these college living spaces "poor." I think they provide a refreshing baseline of equality, helping students from diverse cultural and socioeconomic backgrounds to start their academic journeys on a common footing.

The young Xu family (1987): Mei, her dad, her mom, Tom (Li's husband), and Li.

If my childhood home was modest, it was also an oasis of peace, order, and principle. My parents never openly disagreed or fought about anything, and they never compromised their integrity. During my childhood, a steady stream of comrades knocked on our front door, offering us gifts. I never knew the topic of discussion or why gifts were involved. Later I discovered that despite my parents' humble salaries, they oversaw the hiring and firing of a large cadre of work staff. These gifts were bribes, offered so that my parents might consider someone's uncle or son for one of these coveted positions.

"I'll do my best," my father would say, handing the gifts back, "but please take this with you."

It didn't matter that these simple offerings could have made our lives more comfortable, especially when food was in short supply. My parents modeled an almost Buddhist detachment from our material belongings and life circumstances. I now see their ethical standards and commitment to domestic peace as a priceless gift, one that transformed our existence. We were a tiny boat, it seemed, floating atop a violent sea. Inside this domestic sanctuary, my sister and I enjoyed the illusion that the world itself was an innocent and peaceful place.

Revolutionary Peril and Promise ───────

It may be that my parents cultivated tranquility as a reaction to their own tumultuous upbringings and the suffering of my grandparents. In 1937, Japan invaded China, and the entire country mobilized to thwart this external threat. Immediately following the conclusion of this conflict in 1945, China embarked on four more years of gruesome civil war between the nationalists and communists, culminating in the victory of Chairman Mao's forces, the permanent exile of the nationalists to Taiwan, and the creation of the People's Republic of China (PRC) on the mainland.

PRC officials then seized and redistributed all private land so that wealth would be more evenly dispersed, and so that China might become a society of equals. Drained from years of warfare and foreign occupation, most social classes greeted the communist takeover with cautious optimism. Chinese peasants felt thankful for their newly elevated status, and elites, whose businesses had been seized and whose safety had been comprised by the Japanese, welcomed a new era of peace and stability. Though the PRC seized personal possessions and gradually curtailed individual freedoms, much of the population believed that a fairer and more just society would result.

I wish I knew more about my grandparents and their experiences navigating this turmoil. Prior to the PRC takeover, my maternal grandparents ran a lucrative ceramic business, while my paternal grandfather was a successful sugar and silk merchant. The continuous warfare and the confiscation of property following the liberation means that few photos and no heirlooms or writings from them have survived. They were either lost, destroyed, or consigned to collect dust in a party office somewhere. That was for the best: the fewer items people owned, the less suspect they were. The early communist state even discouraged weddings and funerals, deeming them quaint relics at best and pernicious bourgeois displays of wealth at worst.

Premier Zhou Enlai, one of the PRC's founding fathers, was the closest I had to a grandparent. As towering a figure as Chairman Mao Zedong, Premier Zhou was beloved among Chinese peasants and workers, exercising restraint and saving many from the excesses of Chairman Mao's Cultural Revolution. A handsome and cultured man who'd studied in France, Premier Zhou didn't take advantage of his elite status, advocated for as much freedom as Mao allowed, and was a paragon of humility and leadership. Though I was only nine years old when he died, I still remember the great uncertainty and pangs of loss I felt. Millions filled China's Tiananmen Square and the long boulevard around it, and instead of acknowledging their ancestors in the annual Qingming festival, they paid tribute to this fallen statesman.

My dad was 13 when Premier Zhou helped the Communist Party consolidate control of China. One of six siblings, he fled with his older sister and immediate younger brother two years later, trying to unburden himself from his elite background by making a clean break from his family. He was no different than the other young people of his generation, inspired by the revolutionary promise of liberation from an exploitative system. That generation believed they'd change the world for the better. Joining the navy was my dad's fresh start. Several of his siblings, including his oldest sister, went on to enjoy successful military careers. After attending a select foreign language university, Dad's older sister became a Russian translator, an important role during the early Cold War, when the Soviet-Chinese relationship was strong. But Dad's future would be far more modest, owing not to a lack of intelligence, but of savvy.

I once saw Dad's application for a promotion in the navy and was surprised by how forthcoming he was about his background. The Communist Party had urged such transparency. "Be transparent about your background and you'll receive the best reconciliation," officials suggested. My father disclosed his family's assets as if he were confessing to a priest—the property holdings, down to how many servants they had—hoping to seek atonement for his parents' once elite bourgeois status. Big mistake. The navy transferred him from active duty to a teaching post at what would become a naval academy in the coastal city of Qingdao, located in the eastern province of Shandong. His new job: teach math to would-be naval officers. Like my mother, he never ascended the ranks to leadership and was never consulted for any important management decisions.

I wonder how much my father regretted his youthful naïveté. With his native intelligence, handsome features, and excellent calligraphy, he could have excelled. But he never showed any discouragement and he always fondly seized new opportunities, like when the military later transferred him again to Hangzhou. Like me, he was never too serious, and he always took time to laugh and savor life's joys and simple pleasures. He fondly reminisced about his adventures at sea before he became a teacher, bonded with friends he'd made in the navy, and embraced fun weekend activities like ballroom dancing.

If my dad settled into his military life with relative ease and took adversity in stride, life for my mom was more complicated and challenging. A single child born to a wealthy landowner and merchant, my mother met my father in middle school and only became romantically involved with him later in life. My mom later left her parents and hometown, something she would always regret. Settling in Beijing, she joined the air force and served as a secretary in some capacity. Black-and-white photos of her reveal a beautiful young woman with pitch-black hair styled into two long braids, smiling wholeheartedly into the camera.

Mom later worked as a telephone operator at a Beijing air force command center. Like any young person enthralled in revolutionary fervor, she embraced every task to which she was assigned, including helping out in the kitchen on the weekends. That's how she developed her culinary range, branching out from southern Chinese rice-based staples to northern Chinese delicacies like dumplings. Whether it's preparing the flour or making scrumptious fillings of ground pork, garlic sauce, *pak choi*, or spinach, she can do it all.

In late 1958, when Chairman Mao sent the first wave of "undesirables" to remote parts of northern China for reeducation, Mom was among them. The revolutionary camp where she ended up, comprising young men and women who were either considered nonrevolutionary by birth (unlike farmers and industrial workers) or who questioned Mao's wisdom, was in Heilongjiang, a province bordering Russia. Such a cold, barren location was perfectly suited for people to think hard about their *bad history* and reform. These northern lands are also rich and arable, and though my mother had no farming background, she and her fellow undesirables went to work there, helping China maintain its agricultural independence. Leaving Beijing for the remote north was like moving from New York to the Alaskan hinterland—quite a shock for a woman in her twenties.

During the region's long, cold winters, inhabitants burned whatever wood they could find for warmth. One night, a fire erupted in my mother's dormitory residence, leaving her legs severely burned. In fact, she nearly died. I strongly suspect that her grief-stricken parents were prematurely sickened from almost losing their only child. They both perished in their forties.

When my mom's injury deprived her of independence, my father intervened. They'd kept in touch since high school and had followed one another's military careers. Dad petitioned the Party to marry Mom, offering to save her from a life of government dependence. My parents applied to the military units where they worked, and all agencies agreed that my father could marry a sick woman like my mother (believing she was permanently disabled from the fire). He did have to undergo several evaluations to ensure that he would continue to take her down a revolutionary path.

That's how it worked during the first decade under Chinese communism. The Party not only took control of the market and exercised control in planning macroeconomic policy; it injected itself into the minutia of people's lives, deciding what job you had, where you would live, whom you would marry, where your kids went to nursery school—everything of importance.

Harmony in Hangzhou

In my parents' case, macro and micro forces converged to define their destinies. In the 1950s, when the Korean War concluded and the Cold War began, China remained closed to the outside world and needed to develop its own industry. This first phase of industrialization focused on iron and steel, and Chairman Mao decreed that every major provincial city would have an iron and steel plant to supply China with the metal it needed to build the country's infrastructure and power its military.

In 1959, university personnel asked my father to join his colleagues from the military with education and some management experience to found a large iron and steel mill in the northern suburb of Hangzhou. Dad oversaw a broad range of safety, environmental health, and technology applications at Hangzhou's first iron and steel mill, while my mother taught at the newly established elementary school that exclusively served families of the new mill workers. A preschool, middle, and high school soon followed, ensuring that the mill was a well-supported, self-sustaining organization. As the mill grew to over 10,000 workers, the community of multigenerational families also increased to over 50,000. Mom taught Chinese and math for several years and, thanks to her organizational acumen, later became principal of the elementary school.

My parents made slightly more money than other families because they were considered "intellectuals." My mother's military training gave her the tools she needed to organize teachers, develop common core teaching principles, and design curricula and lesson plans. She oversaw several hundred teachers, who in turn ran classrooms of 40 students (totaling over 3,000 pupils) ranging from 8 to 13 years old. It was an intense role, as many of the teachers hadn't received adequate education in pedagogy and adolescent psychology. My dad's background in management and basic military training similarly showed the Party that he was skilled enough to organize others. Officials therefore appointed him to manage hundreds of millworkers and engineers at the new facility. Such roles weren't particularly desirable, because they were technical, offered no prospect of promotion to leadership ranks, and required grueling six-day work weeks.

Because their roles were so demanding, my parents worked long hours and enjoyed little free time. Dad left our home before sunrise, while Mom stayed up late at night grading homework. With the Party financing housing, healthcare, childcare, and education, most families earned the equivalent of $20 a month.[4] My parents made twice that, mainly because they were retired military veterans with intellectually adjacent occupations. The Party rationed foodstuffs in jin, the Chinese metric equivalent to a half kilogram. I recall one jin of pork—a luxury at the time—costing around 1.8 Yuan, or $0.30. This meant that you could only make such a purchase if these limited meat supplies were available, and then only if you hadn't yet exhausted your monthly rations. While the Soviets rationed bread, the Chinese communists rationed meat as well as rice in the south of the country, and flour for dumplings and noodles in the north. The Party provided everyone with coupons, allocating them 20–30 or so jin of rice or flour and a few jin each of pork per month.[5]

My dad used what little expendable income he had to enrich our lives a bit. When he traveled to nearby Shanghai or big cities like Beijing, he brought home sweetened rice cakes with red bean paste, or White Rabbit candy, a beloved childhood staple because it was rumored to have a real milk base. Having grown up in Guangxi Province, close to Guangdong Province (popularly known as Canton), Mom and Dad naturally gravitated to good food. Long considered China's capital of "haute cuisine," the Cantonese region supports large animal farms, and its tropical climate, with generous rainfall and warm temperatures, nourishes rice paddies and other lush agriculture.[6] Locals prepare traditional dishes, like frog legs atop lotus leaves, salted duck eggs, grilled pigeon, and water spinach with fresh herbs and other flavorings—all steamed or lightly braised so as to retain intricate flavors and delicate tastes.[7] My parents' culinary skills strongly shaped my relationship with food and a love for breaking bread with family and friends, something that has always given me profound joy and meaning.

When he returned from Shanghai, Dad brought me items like cloth dolls and metal kitchen sets. These toys made my already popular sister and me the envy of our peers. Neighborhood children often asked if they could play with our toys, to which we agreed, ensuring us long stretches of enjoyable outdoor playtime.

As a dedicated teacher, my mother sought to do right by her students during a most inhospitable historical moment: the Cultural Revolution. While Mom was supervising teachers and students, Chairman Mao was mobilizing impressionable young Chinese to battle counterrevolutionaries. These bands of youth became his personal proxies, enabling him to consolidate his power and eliminate dissenters, tarring them as "spokesmen for imperialism" or bourgeois supporters of America.

Chairman Mao's Great Proletarian Cultural Revolution focused on social and political purity. By Chairman Mao's logic, if you were educated, you must be bourgeois and therefore counterrevolutionary. A broad swath of professionals, including teachers, professors, doctors, and lawyers, were all plucked out of their roles and sent for reeducation in the countryside. People like my mom took their places. She wasn't as well educated as a professor, but she possessed enough educational and managerial experience to discharge her role.

When someone with my mom's high standards and dedication filled these posts, some teachers grew resentful. Mom hardly enforced rigorous requirements; she simply ensured that teachers arrived on time to teach and either assigned grades to their students or provided them with equivalent forms of feedback. Her staff hated her for this, however, and poisoned the children against her—not that the students needed much encouragement, living in an age when teachers were already suspect and considered sorely in need of reeducation.

"Principal Lin!" one of the teachers would say to a student, referring to my mom. "She told us that we should give you this bad grade."

"Principal Lin said you shouldn't go home today because you have to make up your exams."

This widespread anti-intellectualism and disrespect for authority hit us hard. I remember students throwing stones at our house and breaking windows. My mom was stalwart and simply shrugged her shoulders. "Never mind them, they're just kids," she observed.

Meanwhile, my dad's job was physically exhausting. Iron and steel mills use coal to heat furnaces, and in the early days, accidents abounded. Dad was always the first to arrive on scene, sometimes taking control without any protective garments or equipment. He'd then stay, and following any accidents, console any families who had lost a relative or who now had to care for someone rendered permanently disfigured.

When Dad was diagnosed with Alzheimer's at the age of 65, the doctors suspected that his extensive brain damage came from exposure to mercury, lead, and other industrial toxins present in the mill. Whether or not that was true, this much is certain: the Party couldn't have done a better job in selecting my parents for their roles. They were pillars of integrity, risking bodily injury and enduring routine humiliation all for humble pay and treatment alike.

But they could also be whimsical and fun. One day, when I was seven or eight years old, I told my dad I wanted to take a train ride. I'd never done so before, and in retrospect this was the beginning of my love affair with travel.

"Where are we going?" my dad asked.

He was to choose the destination, I said, as I would accompany him anywhere.

We went to the train station, and he purchased two tickets to Jiaxing, a little town nestled between Shanghai and Hangzhou that's famous for its bamboo-wrapped zongzi—sticky rice dumplings filled with soy flavored pork, chestnuts, sweet red bean, Chinese dates, and the like. Upon arrival, Dad and I visited the city's most renowned purveyor of zongzi and returned home with some goodies. This brief father-daughter trip marks the beginning of my life-long passion for travel.

When Dad and I returned home, beaming with happiness, we saw Mom's curious look.

"Where did you go?" she asked.

"We can't tell you," I responded, "Or you'll be mad."

My military-minded father might have indulged me, but he was no aesthete. During my early childhood, he cut my hair himself in a blunt and uneven bowl cut. "The left is too high," he'd observe, and then try to even it out, only making the other side disproportionate. He kept cutting to even it out until my hair fell at the middle of my ears, making me resemble a mushroom. Most kids would have let this go, but even at four or five, I was outraged and protested. Tears streamed down my face as I imagined the boys at my school mercilessly taunting me. That was my first fight with my dad. In retrospect, it was also the first sign of my budding fashion style.

My mom had excellent taste and explored it within the limited confines of the time by hiring a tailor. That meant that even if we lacked in extravagance and variety of clothing, everything fit well. She also personally tailored each of my garments from an early age or made them from scratch. When I later left for boarding school and started to explore my creative side, I kept this great introduction to tailoring with me. Armed with photographs from a magazine or pictures in my head, I'd venture to stores selling men's fabrics. Everybody always wondered where I acquired my clothes because they weren't available in stores. The trick was good tailoring.

During my boarding school years, when I commuted home on Saturday afternoons, I saw the first flowering of fashion percolating in China. This came in the form of original equipment manufacturing (OEM) workshops that processed and executed orders exactly as a client requested. Rejected merchandise from larger companies, referred to as "gray goods," began circulating at the time, too. All I know about these fashions was that they diverged from the daily uniforms of my parents and were therefore exciting. Rather than going home directly, I spent two or three hours at these bus stop shops, wandering among the pop-up booths. I was always the first to try something new, like denim jeans or pedal pushers. Other girls joined me on these shopping excursions, asking me for fashion opinions, or for me to select outfits for them.

It wasn't long before my openness to novelty got me in trouble. One day, my school principal summoned me to his office, pointed to my jeans, and said, "Mei, you cannot wear this representation of capitalist clothing."

"What capitalist?" I responded. "This is what cowboys wear in America and they're working class."

Certain fashion statements, music choices, and other cultural decisions were easily judged as bourgeois and capitalist. As I was transitioning into my middle school years, we started to hear music from our enemy Taiwan. People began humming these popular songs about Western love and romance. It was a small sign that China was opening, even if most people condemned the themes expressed in these ballads.

Unlike fashion and music, food was a safe indulgence—a place to express non-suspect creativity, and something that was precious to us because of its scarcity. Food also figured prominently in my relationship with my older sister, Li, my only sibling. Li was and has remained a towering pillar in my life. Our two personalities were almost embedded in our names themselves. In Chinese, Li means "power and strength" and, true to form, my sister was bold, socially outspoken, and a dominant personality. If anyone was destined to become a leader and entrepreneur, it was Li. Tellingly, Mei means "plum blossom." I was more delicate and a less forceful presence than Li, and growing up I was always referred to as "Li's little sister." Some people still refer to me that way.

Li's preeminence seemed fated because, as she never tired of reminding me, she was the promising child and I was her "insurance policy." At around three or four years old, she was misdiagnosed and almost died from meningitis. She was so sick my mom worried there might be something wrong with her brain, and that's why they planned to conceive a second child. My sister might have made that story up, but I doubt it. She overheard our parents discussing many important matters, and I suspect that she eavesdropped on this one when she was around four or five years old. (Of course, this was before the one-child policy came into effect, but long after the government encouraged families to bear many children.)

Li is naturally intelligent and possesses impressive social skills. She also seems to contain many layers, while I'm much more one-dimensional. Since girls mature early, and since she had over five years and significant social intelligence on me, she's always understood things better than me.

Aware of her potential, my sister's teachers chose her to telegraph "power and strength" in school performances and speeches. My parents sensed her talent, too, and when she turned 17, they trained me, her 11-year-old sibling, to prepare Li's meals so she could devote her spare time to studying for university entrance exams. Imagine these entrance exams like the SATs, only significantly harder.

During that time at home Li created household drama of her own, and as she reached her teenage years, she started secretly seeing a boy. Social convention of the time labeled such activity as politically incorrect and bourgeois. Li and Dad fought about this, and I remember him yelling at the top of his lungs, frightening me. I tried to thwart such conflict, covering for my sister if she was out, telling my parents that she was busy studying with a friend instead of spending time with a boy. At 10 or 11, I served as Li's keeper as well as her cook, proactively chasing her around town so that I could know her whereabouts and better craft the stories I told my parents on her behalf. Unbeknownst to us all, hiding and pretending was gradually becoming a family tradition. This practice matured and festered into a larger habit for me as I studiously avoided conflicts and uncomfortable situations in my marriage and professional life.

After becoming the self-appointed leader at home, ensuring that domestic harmony between my father and sister continued at all costs, I put these interpersonal skills to work at school. Noticing that you didn't have to be the tallest or strongest in class to assume leadership, I never felt intimidated by other kids. What I lacked in physical strength, I made up for with a steady and calm authority that somehow always prompted my classmates to follow the rules. My elementary school teachers noticed my organizational acumen (or maybe just that I liked taking charge and bossing people around) and took advantage. If my math or Chinese teachers knew they'd be tardy to class, they'd appoint me interim class leader, and I went to work reminding students to finish their homework and prepare their lessons. Before I knew it, I was organizing practices and after-school singing and dancing performances for a whole grade of 300 students. The boys were sometimes rowdy, naughty, and confrontational, but I still ensured that they queued in line and calmed down.

Hogwarts Bound

Near the end of elementary school, I took a standardized examination administered to all of Hangzhou's children competing for entry into a new, selective middle school. My teachers told me about this new school in the area geared toward foreign language learning, but I didn't know what that meant. All I knew was that the older I became, the more academic challenges I embraced and the more confident I grew in my own abilities. I subtly resented existing in my sister's shadow, having to carry her burden and comply with her demands simply because I was younger. When the opportunity came to embark on a new adventure, I embraced it, somehow knowing that it would help me craft my own identity.

By this time, China was perceptibly opening to the rest of the world. Seven years earlier (1972), President Richard Nixon made a historic visit to the PRC, marking the first time America's leader had visited the country since the 1949 revolution.[8] Nixon called it "the week that changed the world," and he was right: it heralded a new era of Sino-American economic and cultural relations that persists into the present day. Four years later, in September 1976, Chairman Mao died, enabling the Party, with Deng Xiaoping at the helm, to pivot away from isolationism to a more pragmatic internationalism, and from a centralized economy to "market socialism."[9]

Since China couldn't become a global power without more career-trained diplomats, it decided to open eight elite preparatory schools to train a new cadre of foreign service officials. Competition for entry was keen. Every school in Hangzhou, nominated several of its top students to sit for the entrance exam. Only a select handful of those students advanced to a grueling round of oral exams. During these interviews, we recounted Chinese stories, summarized key reading points, and attempted to repeat long English sentences, our accuracy and recall with this foreign-sounding gibberish suggesting promise for future language acquisition. I've always had a great memory, and I'm good at extemporaneous thinking, so I did well.

At the age of 12, almost one year after China had promulgated its famous Open Door policy, I joined the first cohort of students in China's elite foreign language middle school.[10] It was thrilling to think I'd be moving to a boarding school and living, sleeping, and learning with a group of kids my own age. Unfortunately, that initial excitement evaporated as I found myself unprepared for the academic challenge. I'd always been the top student in elementary school and never worked too hard to excel. But when I arrived at my new English-immersive learning environment, I trailed my peers, some of whom were children of professors and other professionals and had some English-speaking experience.

During my first year I earned As and Bs in most subjects but was failing in English reading, writing, and listening comprehension. Our classes were small, never exceeding 18 children, and so despite my small stature, I couldn't hide. When the teachers called my name, I was overcome with stress and froze, forgetting the answer entirely or mangling the pronunciation.

I knew that failure lay ahead if I continued, so I adopted a new strategy. Whenever the teacher posed a question to any student in any class, I answered it. I modulated my voice so as not to distract the other students, but the teachers could still hear me. Gradually, instead of listening to the student they'd called on, they focused completely on me. In effect, I received one-on-one coaching for an entire semester. The teachers saw my eagerness and hunger for knowledge and responded with extra help. I became one of the best students in the class, growing more confident even with language.

Though I lacked foreign language experience, I intuitively knew that learning a language was fundamentally different than science. You can't master a language through logic and formulas alone. You must also approach it creatively, making up stories and play-acting imaginative scenarios, all the while allowing yourself to commit many errors and fumble out loud. I spent extra time listening to grainy recordings on the school's tape recorders, painstakingly trying to master English pronunciation and intonation (much to the detriment of my long-term hearing). As a reward, I gained access to English literature, devouring books like *Little Women* and *Jane Eyre* and reciting poems and excerpts from *Great Expectations*.

From Monday to Saturday each week, I studied intensely with my cohort of middle schoolers and only briefly returned to family life on Saturday evening. In the 1980s, everyone used bicycles and public transportation to get around, and my commute to and from school was about 90 minutes, involving two bus rides and a bicycle. Every Monday morning for six years, my dad hoisted me onto the back of his bike, where I sat sideways as he peddled me to the bus stop. Sometimes we were silent, and sometimes he asked how I was.

"Do you have enough to eat at school?" he often asked.

In truth, I was constantly hungry, just like the rest of my classmates. During the time when my body was rapidly growing from the ages of 12 to 18, China was struggling to feed its large population and had to ration core nutritional staples like meat. We typically ate a breakfast of Chinese steamed bread with cereal and preserved cabbages. On lucky days, we might get an egg. This humble meal had to last until lunch hour at noon, when we'd get a modest serving of tofu, vegetables, and, if we were lucky, some minced pork and white rice. Dinner was modest, too—some pork, green vegetables, and more steamed rice.

I looked forward to those dinners a lot, but by the time I'd finished waiting in line, the meat had usually vanished, and only vegetables and juice remained. So, on my bike, I'd tell my dad the truth: yes, I was hungry, and I would love some candy or snacks. The following week, he'd hand me a paper bag full of treats like White Rabbit candy or black sesame clusters with sugar.

Many of the kids also returned to school with food to supplement our modest cafeteria offerings. In the evenings, I'd hear students stirring under the bedspreads, eating food they'd brought from home. That extra food never lasted long! One day out of six each week, school authorities let us venture to the little town in which our campus was situated and buy some snacks. My adolescent body craved pure chocolate. I'd devour it entirely before I arrived back at school.

I once craved chocolate so badly that I purchased some outside of the sanctioned time each week. I threw the chocolate bar over the fence and then climbed over myself, only to find one of my teachers glaring at me. "What is this, Mei? You're a leader in your class and grade. But how can we trust you if you break our rules and bring extra food?"

This was a rare moment of rebellion. I hardly ever broke the rules, much less complained or advocated for myself. Though this entire experiment in training young leaders was new and poorly designed for adolescents, complaining wasn't part of the culture—at school, at home, or in society in general. The school building was old, and some nights we'd hear mice scurrying around in our shoes and shrug it off. We also could barely fit on adult chairs and tables, and we often spent our dinner time walking around the track, eating our food as we went.

We may have lacked in creature comforts, but we enjoyed learning in abundance. For the first time in decades, foreign nationals journeyed to China to teach English in schools like ours. Hailing from Australia, Canada, and New Zealand, many were universally welcomed in a rapidly opening China. These teachers were young and passionate about the school's mission, and they exposed us to diverse cultures and accents.

Chinese faculty members also served as our surrogate parents, taking turns supervising us in the evenings as we did homework at our desks. When we had questions, they'd patiently respond. They almost never scolded us in public and instead provided us corrections individually. Enabled by a 1:3 faculty-to-student ratio, such attention was invaluable, especially when it came to mastering English. I would never have found a job in the United States, let alone had the confidence to become an entrepreneur, without the communication abilities they helped inculcate.

One of my teachers, Ms. Shang Xiaomin, was a slight exception to this trend. During my early failures with English, she was harsh and broke with protocol as she corrected me in front of the entire class. But the more she embarrassed me, the more I strove to improve. It was just the pressure that I needed. During my second year at school, after I began excelling at English, she took me aside and said, "I hope you understand that I had to do this. There was no other way to correct you."

Years later, I'd meet her when she traveled to the United States as an exchange teacher. "You were one of my favorite turnaround stories," she told me. "You were the smallest child, sitting right in front, and no one could intimidate you."

Our school screened movies like *Out of Africa, Gone with the Wind,* and *The Godfather*. They also offered us more mundane Western cultural staples, like a textbook called *English This Way* that depicted American families living in their own homes with technological marvels called refrigerators. These boxes prolonged the life of food by maintaining it at cool temperatures. Instead of going to the market every day and painstakingly washing and peeling fruit and vegetables as we did, American families could remove the goods from the refrigerator or even harvest them from room-temperature cans. This struck us as magical. Refrigerators, home ownership, unlimited supplies of meat, chocolate cake, the absence of food rations and long lines at the market—these all showed us how luxurious life could be.

Other experiences, like watching the 1979 legal drama *Kramer vs. Kramer*, exposed us to different lifestyle options. This movie dramatized a divorcing couple with a young son, showing how the parents negotiated custody and related issues. But at the time in China there were few divorces, and we were all confused at first. Little did I know how my life would change, and how I'd struggle with divorce and co-parenting decades later.

My expanding cultural horizons changed my relationships with my parents and sister. We inhabited different worlds, and gradually stopped our daily communications. Reading the classics of Western literature, and in the original English no less, also distinguished me from my sister, who had little interest in them, gravitating as she did toward science, Chinese literature, and calligraphy. Growing up, she'd been such a great writer that I'd even copy her sentences and try to emulate them. But now that I was reading hundreds of novels, my English surpassed hers considerably, to the point where she began to brag about me to her friends. "My sister is at this new school," she said. "They speak English and have foreign teachers." I'd earned my sister's respect and our relationship gradually became more egalitarian.

During summer breaks when I was home from school, I'd withdraw and immerse myself in the fictional worlds of novels. And, for the first time, I began to yearn for more material things. Several years earlier, when televisions arrived in China, my parents instituted strict screen times for Li and me, much like parents do today. By this time, some of our neighbors had learned how to game the system and earn some additional money on the side. I didn't resent lacking a television of our own, but I noticed that others had generated surplus income and I thought it might be nice to have some extra food, in addition to luxuries like a television.

As our time at boarding school ended, my fellow students and I fretted about where we'd end up. I knew I wanted to be a diplomat. That initial longing I had as a child upon seeing the Cambodian royalty on a state visit had matured into a keen desire to represent my country abroad. I wanted to shake hands with other foreign dignitaries and work with them on important bilateral or multilateral initiatives. In China, however, everyone's destiny hinges on standardized examinations. I'd survived these examinations thus far, but my fate still rested on how I did on the dreaded National College Entrance Examination, known as the *gaokao*.

The *gaokao* had been suspended for over a decade during the tumult of the Cultural Revolution.[11] Following Chairman Mao's death, Premier Deng Xioping returned to power, vanquished his enemies (known as the Gang of Four), and made education a central plank in his policy platform. Midway through boarding school, in the autumn of 1977, Party leaders reinstated the *gaokao*. Academically inclined students, who'd been sent to rural outposts for reeducation on agricultural communes, reacted to the news with glee and struggled to find textbooks and remember mathematical equations. Some had even faked workplace injuries to buy themselves extra study time. The *New York Times* described that initial examination as likely "the most competitive scholastic test in modern Chinese history," and the fortunate 4.7 percent of those admitted to the class of '77 as China's very best talent.[12] Seven years later (1984), and a year prior to graduation, I prepared to sit for that harrowing examination, too.

My schoolmates and I were more prepared than most to excel on these tests, having diligently studied with an eye toward those exams since 1979. Nonetheless, perhaps we had overestimated the meritocratic nature of the Chinese system. During our senior year, several officials from the Ministry of Foreign Affairs visited our school and interviewed some of the male candidates. They sought four male students to bypass the exams, enroll in more courses in foreign countries, and then assume diplomatic posts in embassies. The girls were upset because our English was generally stronger than the boys'. But it was the boys who evaded the dreaded college entrance exam and embarked on exciting careers in the foreign service.

My disappointment eased somewhat when I learned that several elite universities planned to visit our school and admit some of us directly. It was a thrilling prospect, akin to receiving admission to your dream school without having to take the SATs or write admission essays.

The school invited me to interview for Beijing Foreign Studies University, the institution that offers the most comprehensive foreign language education in China and produces the most Chinese diplomats. I was extremely nervous on the day of the interview, but when the college representative began conversing with me in an American accent, she immediately put me at ease. I'd already immersed myself so thoroughly in American culture, literature, and pronunciation that I radiated confidence.

After a few days passed, one of my teachers gave me the good news: Mei was accepted! Thrilled, I basked in the moment. I'd worked diligently day and night for five years, and now it had all paid off. A few weeks later, our teachers told us to move our desks from our classroom and quietly pack up our books and notes so as not to disturb the students still preparing for the *gaokao*. So ended our steady six-year march toward college.

My mom and dad were delighted because any university in Beijing was highly prestigious, and I was going to one that produced Chinese ambassadors. In September 1985, when I was 18 years old, I joined four other classmates—two girls and two boys—to receive collegiate language training in Beijing. Our reputation preceded us, and everyone referred to Emily, Jennifer, and Mei, the females of the group, as "the three flowers from Hangzhou." We all came from a region famed for its beauty, and they expected us to be beautiful and graceful, too. The three Hangzhou flowers blossomed even more in Beijing, and we've remained friends to this day.

Beijing Bound

When I began college in September 1985, I found Beijing a bleak and unattractive city. Imagine a large, boxy urban area with grand boulevards of 5–10 lanes in each direction. When it came to urban planning and architecture, the city had adopted Soviet models, meaning large brutalist concrete buildings that lacked style and intimacy. In the winter and early spring, sand from Mongolia's Gobi Desert blew through the streets, sometimes whipping our faces, especially when we traveled by bicycle. The winters were harsh and long, and the coal-burning stoves encased the city in soot.

Despite its aesthetic disadvantages, Beijing was a place of immense opportunity, and it expanded my horizons even further. During my first year, I lived with four other girls in a dorm. One of them was Chinese American and had just returned from the United States to visit her parents, who were teaching at a university. Having grown up in the West, she didn't look or think like us at all. Unfortunately, she suffered from bulimia, and we called the hospital several times when her heart became too weak to support her undernourished body. She might have been a dancer; with the constant stream of roommates and classmates coming and going each year, I can't remember for sure. But I do remember that a poster of a beautiful ballerina hung over her bed, emblazoned with a quote: "If you can dream it, you can become it." I'd soon lose track of this roommate, but that quotation has stayed with me, serving as a personal mantra, a guiding life principle.

Because I had arrived academically prepared, I was able to take advantage of Beijing's many opportunities. I soon discovered that I could skip school and no one would notice. I could also complete all the exams without studying too hard. My most academically enriching experience came from an intensive "college internship" that showed me how much I enjoyed working in a multicultural environment.

Early in my freshman year, a sociology professor from Dartmouth College, who was teaching in Beijing on an exchange program that year, took me aside. She and her Austrian husband dazzled me because they worked in different continents and had adopted two African American children. They were about as progressive and cool as I could imagine, and one night, when they hosted several faculty and students for dinner, she had an idea. "You should talk to my husband," she said, referring to her spouse, who worked for the World Bank in Beijing. "They really need good interpreters and translators." Thus began my association with the World Bank, and the United Nations Development Programme (UNDP) with which it partnered, which would last my entire college experience.

Unlike odd jobs I'd had in the past, like tutoring English to children of wealthy parents, my position at the World Bank gave me a purpose, mission, and connection to a grand cause. In this case, the larger mission was to help developing countries with infrastructure, energy, and transparency in governance. To that end, I accompanied the organization's experts and consultants on 10-day missions devoted to helping communities grapple with environmental protection, water, sanitation, electricity, and the like. Unlike my university classes, this was a real challenge. Picture a room of 40 people—20 English speakers on one side, 20 Mandarin speakers on the other—with me in the middle, breathlessly translating between the two.

I'm being generous when I say, "English speakers." Imagine Scandinavians with thick northern accents speaking about best practices in sanitation to other experts with strong Thai accents. In this dynamic, international environment, I had to master new vocabulary related to reservoirs, latrines, and hydroelectricity. I also learned another, not-so-healthy skill: I perfected the art of eating quickly. Since I was the only one who could speak in both languages, I spent much of mealtime helping the consultants and engineers understand one another. This obligation left me precious few minutes to inhale my food before attendants came to clear it. To my lasting regret, this habit followed me to America. Today I eat with such efficiency that when most of my fellow diners are working on their appetizers, I'm ready to attack my dessert.

In 1986, I joined a World Bank/UNDP mission to inner Mongolia and boarded my first airplane. It was a rickety Soviet turboprop, but that didn't concern me. What did concern me, shortly after takeoff, was my stomach. I vomited the entire time. I was seated next to John Karlbermatten, a kind gentleman and longtime department head at the bank's Washington, DC, headquarters. He bore the brunt of my motion sickness. "Don't look around, just look at the head of the person in front of you," he cautioned while collecting paper airsick bags from the surrounding passengers. Despite this initial unpleasantness, he would become an unfailing mentor and close friend.

In 1987, I accompanied representatives of the World Bank and the UNDP on a much more exciting mission to northwest China. We'd spent a lot of time in the poor areas of China. But our destination now—the city of Kashgar, near the countries of Afghanistan, Pakistan, Kirghizstan, and Tajikistan, and home to a good number of China's Muslim Uighurs—made the strongest impression on me. The place lacked basic infrastructure, and so the World Bank's mission was to build latrines. When we landed, I was struck by the aridity, the dirt, and the sight of gorgeous, dark-complexioned children sitting along the road. One child was especially adorable, and after greeting him I touched his face. It was then I realized that these children weren't dark skinned; they were caked in dirt. In Chinese culture, it's impolite to touch the faces of children, but these kids were so welcoming that they put me at ease.

These children marked the highlight of the trip, and the meals marked the low point. Unfortunately, every meal involved lamb. Cured lamb for breakfast, lamb stew for lunch, and lamb chops for dinner. I poked around my plate for some naan bread, but I couldn't eat much because lamb revolts me. I found out much later that I am a "super-taster," which means that I have more taste buds, by volume, than most people. After several days had elapsed, I began to feel weak, and I begged the kitchen staff for a change of menu: "Can you do me a favor? Could you make me some chicken soup?

"Oh, no," they replied. "We have something better. A whole lamb for dinner."

I politely told them that as lovely as the lamb sounded, I only wanted some chicken. When dinner arrived that evening, one kitchen attendant brought me some chicken soup. Everyone stopped talking and dropped their forks and knives, following the chicken with their eyes. Apparently, the entire group was fed up with eating three courses of lamb each day, too, and when my boss and my bosses' boss looked so happy to see the chicken, I passed some around for them to enjoy as well.

After spending several days in the area, it was clear that the World Bank hadn't asked the locals what they needed when crafting the mission. Their dry climate put them in great need of water pumps. "When we poo," they explained, "it's so dry that it turns to powder in several hours." Latrines were optional for this community, but water wasn't. They didn't have enough to drink, let alone bathe their children. I was too young and inexperienced to object to the mission, but it struck me as wrong that we couldn't host a community meeting and allow people to air their own needs. Although China owes a great debt to the World Bank for its development initiatives, the organization is structured like a large bureaucracy that is hierarchical and not always interested in soliciting, let alone prioritizing, local needs. It was such awareness of the limits of established institutions, the notion that there had to be a better way of doing things, that would one day inspire me to become an entrepreneur.

At around this time, in the summer of my freshman year, I met my future husband, David, at an intercollegiate summer camp in Beidaihe, an exclusive beach resort several hundred kilometers from Beijing. A dedicated physics student, David attended Beijing University, the Harvard of China, and that summer had decided to serve as a counselor at this camp. My more estrogen-heavy school, specializing in foreign language, gravitated to science boys like him. Strikingly handsome and with elite pedigree, David stood above the rest (quite literally, as he was much taller than most Chinese boys). Five years my senior, he was already a graduate student and possessed a certain melancholy and mystery that attracts happy and outgoing girls like me. His charm and charisma immediately won me over, though I was aware of all the other girls who were eagerly trying to engage him, too.

I was completely unprepared to pursue a man like David. Growing up under the shadow of my towering sister, Li, and with parents who never complimented my looks, I was unsure of my appearance and doubted my physical attractiveness. I let the thought of David drift off as I left the camp and returned home to spend the rest of the summer with my family.

A young Mei and David taking a break from studies at Beijing University (1988).

In 1986, when the fall semester of my sophomore year began, I saw David again at my university because he'd enrolled in an international trade course. He asked me out and I said yes to what would become my first relationship—and it was exciting. Every weekend, we ventured out on our bikes, exploring Beijing in the cold. In the depths of winter, I rode on the back of David's bicycle, just like I had done with my dad, and we visited city parks buried in snow. Over northwestern staples like ramen noodles in beef broth and spicy and delicious chicken kabab, we discussed our future dreams and the possibility of studying overseas together.

By this time, the public pursuit of wealth in China was becoming more commonplace and culturally accepted. My friends started cultivating sugar daddies and dating taxi drivers because of their affluence. Yes, you read that correctly. As some of the first independent contractors in China, taxi drivers were on the bleeding edge of Sino capitalism. Most everyone still worked for state-owned companies and netted a similar salary. But when you drove a taxi, you were your own boss and you kept the change. Suddenly, many of my female schoolmates were trying to better their social station by cozying up to taxi drivers.

Part-time work at the World Bank provided me a considerable advantage. When I tallied my earnings each week, I found I was making 10 times more than my mom earned in her demanding, full-time teaching job. I started presenting my parents with gifts, treating my dad to chocolate, a polo shirt, or a meal at a nice restaurant. In China, gift-giving is much more prevalent than in the United States, where people typically only gift close family members or lovers. Chinese people give presents freely and often. Later on in America, I would gift my colleagues some perfume from a trip and they thought I was either crazy or harboring a romantic fantasy about them.

My parents were proud of me and my well-paid, high-status job, but they worried about my relationship with David because I was so young and inexperienced. My sister and I both married too young, but my parents were from a generation in which they didn't coach us about relationships. I wish they'd told us it was perfectly acceptable to have a relationship that didn't end in marriage. But during this time in China there was still a stigma about young women who broke off relationships.

This naïveté about relationships is something that I've shared with Emily and Jennifer, the other two Hangzhou flowers. Emily now lives in France, and Jennifer splits her time between Hong Kong and New York. We've thrived in our adult lives but have all later reflected on how our top-rate educations left us unschooled in the ways of the world. We all can't imagine a better laboratory to master English and train diplomats, but interacting with so many like-minded kids didn't expose us to the complexity of people and relationships. Of the 55 graduates of our high school class, only a handful have been spared divorce.

Despite the demands of a nearly full-time job at the World Bank and my burgeoning romance, I managed to enjoy the vibrance of Beijing, a city that was then experiencing a cultural and technological flowering. I joined the city's youth in approaching the world with curiosity and wonder. English Corners emerged in the public parks as places where people shared their understanding of the world while practicing English. My English was strong and my personality engaging, making me a favorite at these places. The topic of our conversations gradually trended toward foreign companies like IBM and 3M and domestic entrepreneurship, a subject of great interest to a generation sensing a climate of increased possibility and openness. New technology companies like Stone came of age at this time, as the first wave of Sino capitalism began to extend beyond taxi drivers.

Market experimentation initially surfaced near Hong Kong, where people became independent entrepreneurs, transforming obsolete and uncompetitive state-owned enterprises. By the late 1980s, most of mainland China exported goods internationally. The economy boomed, and the country began building highways and other infrastructure to allow for exports to reach these markets. Such growth generated both excitement and uncertainty. People began expressing their resentment at the government for playing favorites with party elites. In China, we have a saying: "When you are hungry, you aren't thinking about a lot, but when you have money, you start to wonder." As my generation began to flirt with a different life, we began to dream about all the possibilities that the vast and multicultural world had to offer.

This is probably what stoked my dreams of working in the foreign service, and I enrolled in many American studies and foreign affairs classes. Though I was never enmeshed in the academic and social life of my school, my location in Beijing's "university district," home to about a hundred universities, felt like one giant Chinese Stanford. I watched Chinese computing get its start and technology giants like Lenovo take off. Other people spotted market needs and capitalized on them. A schoolmate of David's noticed that for ambitious Chinese students to succeed, they needed to master standardized English examinations like the TOEFL, GRE, or GMAT. He began a practice service called the New Oriental Education & Technology Group Inc., which became a national sensation and eventually went public on the NASDAQ. This wasn't a culture of making quick money. It was a brand of youth-led entrepreneurship as universities and businesses worked synergistically to translate abstract ideas into serviceable technologies.

Unlike other national capitals (Washington, DC, comes to mind), Beijing was also a cultural capital. I enjoyed its professional ballet performances and orchestras, as well as photography exhibits, movies, and museums. I couldn't always afford tickets, but I could stroll by galleries and see contemporary Chinese art coming into its own, reviving from the slumber of the Cultural Revolution. Fashion, I routinely observed, was still lacking, but students were beginning to modestly embrace Western ideas of free speech and personal expression. David's Beijing University was on the vanguard of progressive ideas, producing some of the country's celebrated thinkers, economists, and historians. At his school, there was a wall on which students could post their reflections and ideas, like a primitive version of Twitter. People posted elaborate and passionate messages at night under the cover of darkness, and the next morning students and faculty gathered around, curious to take it all in.

As college graduation approached in 1989, and I was busy traveling for the World Bank and taking my final examinations, Beijing basked in a warm spring. April marks Chinese Memorial Day, when people frequent parks and sweep ancestral tombs. That's right: you clean up the environment around your family tombs, burning incense and candles and adorning these memorials with flowers and fruit. China had just lost President Hu Yaobang, a beloved statesman who was among the first generation of soldiers fighting alongside China's fathers.

We all know the events of June 1989, which changed the lives of millions, including me. After Tiananmen Square, the World Bank and foreign embassies left the country, former allies levied sanctions, and foreign leaders, including Soviet General Secretary Mikhail Gorbachev, denounced China.[13] With the embassies closed and the economy suffering, my dream of becoming a diplomat was officially "on hold." I followed many recent graduates and began work in a mineral export warehouse in Dalian, one of China's major port cities, located close to the Korean peninsula in the North.

I moved to Dalian in early September 1989, when the weather was already frigid. With its nice beaches and seafood, the area was known for its beauty, though while I was there it was too cold to enjoy the coast, and I never sampled any of the fish. In the late 1980s, China exported choice seafood abroad and the government didn't allocate decent food to incoming workers. This was especially the case for my rebellious generation. After one meal there, I knew the food would be bad. Dalian residents consume flour products, so we ate steamed buns (made of basic white flour and yeast) and thin rice porridge. Lunch was a small meal without much nutrition. You might get some preserved cabbages and eggs and, if you were lucky, a little bit of dried fish or some meat on the weekend. The short supply of bland food remined me of boarding school.

I had blossomed as an amateur chef in Beijing, feasting on steamed fish, braised pork ribs, and fresh, stir-fried vegetables. Preparing food had been a relaxing and spiritual grounding for me, and now, as I ate steamed white buns consisting only of flour and yeast, I felt lost and deeply unsatisfied. When I turned 22 that September, hunger gnawed away at me, as I dreamed of my mom's homemade Cantonese dumplings along with White Rabbit candy and those dark chocolate bars of my youth.

In addition to physical hunger, I was ravenous for intellectual stimulation. The warehouse at which I worked was in a city suburb, so every day I boarded a bus for 45 minutes, watching the dull scenery pass by until I arrived at the single-level structure equipped with one desk and two chairs. From morning to evening each day I'd sit or stand inside the structure along with my supervisor, a very quiet chain-smoking man in his forties who didn't speak a word.

Once each morning a truck arrived to retrieve a load of the minerals for export, which I acknowledged with a check on my clipboard. In the afternoon, another truck arrived, and I supplied another checkmark. That was it: two truckloads a day. There was nothing else to do, and no phones, computers, books, or conversation to distract me.

At the end of the first month, I made the difficult decision to quit my job, return to Beijing, and venture to America to study. This dream would prove daunting because it required me to find my own way in the slowly emerging, hypercompetitive private sector. My mom and dad were frightened because they'd worked in the public sector their entire lives. There's a stigma about resigning government posts—once you do, you look suspicious or defective, and it's hard to secure one again. They feared I might be making a huge mistake. All I knew was that staying here would break my body and spirit, and that I somehow needed to reclaim a sense of purpose and dignity.

I spent the next year struggling to collect my paperwork and my finances to make a move. If I wanted to secure a passport to study overseas anytime soon, I'd have to pay the Chinese government back for the free tuition it had generously lavished on me. That tuition was provided with the expectation that I would dedicate five years of hard work in China. In order to leave before fulfilling this state obligation, I'd have to drain all the savings that I had accumulated from the World Bank and borrow money from my relatives. This sum, around 10,000 renminbi in 1989, was vast, particularly given that underpaid state employees like my parents (who were helping) earned 150–200 renminbi a month. I'll never forget the day that I had managed to amass the money. There were no checking accounts or credit cards at the time, and so all I had was a big collection of 100 renminbi bills. I gathered them all in a plastic trash bag instead of a purse, so that I wouldn't be robbed. I biked with that money to my university and watched the lady behind the counter count it out, one stack at a time.

I had purchased a new life.

- Do you want to be an entrepreneur but are not sure what type of business to start? Look back at your early life and see any patterns and affinities that emerge, like my love of fashion.
- What forms of adversity did you encounter in your early life? Use these formative experiences to your advantage. Entrepreneurial success requires grit and resiliency.
- Identify some of the most important relationships from your youth. How would you draw on them, practically or as inspiration, in your current or future business?
- All entrepreneurship ultimately rests on awareness of the outside world and a desire to impact it. My distance from the outside world as a child made me even more alert to social and cultural trends. What types of influences might have affected your perception of the world and how might you leverage such influences in a business setting?

Endnotes

1. James Zheng Gao, *The Communist Takeover of Hangzhou: The Transformation of City and Cadre, 1949–1954* (Honolulu: University of Hawai'i Press, 2004), 219.
2. Ibid., 231, 243.
3. Ibid., 227–229.
4. This is based on my recollection.
5. These are my best recollections and seem to accord with scholarly estimates as well. See, Ralph W. Huenemann, "Urban Rationing in Communist China," *China Quarterly*, no. 26 (April–June 1966): 48, https://www.jstor.org/stable/651610.
6. "Why Cantonese Food Is the World's Favourite Chinese Cuisine," *China Tours*, updated May 26, 2020, https://www.chinatours.com/catonese-cuisine/.
7. Ibid., "Why Cantonese Food Is the World's Favourite." Also based on my personal recollections of this regional cuisine.
8. Andrew Glass, "President Nixon Arrives in China, Feb. 21, 1972," *Politico*, February 21, 2016, https://www.politico.com/story/2016/02/president-nixon-arrives-in-china-feb-21-1972-219444.

9. A. Doak Barnett, "Ten Years After Mao," *Foreign Affairs,* Fall 1986, https://www.foreignaffairs.com/articles/asia/1986-09-01/ten-years-after-mao.

10. "Open Door Policy," BBC, accessed March 5, 2020, http://news.bbc.co.uk/2/shared/spl/hi/in_depth/china_politics/key_people_events/html/8.stm.

11. David Lague, "1977 Exam Opened Escape Route into China's Elite," *New York Times,* January 6, 2008, https://www.nytimes.com/2008/01/06/world/asia/06china.html.

12. Ibid.

13. "Tiananmen Square Protests," History, updated May 31, 2020, https://www.history.com/topics/china/tiananmen-square.

2

AMERICAN ODYSSEY

In January 1991, when I first set foot on American soil, I thought I'd arrived on another planet. That's because, as I deplaned at Washington, DC's Dulles International Airport and shuffled through the terminal, I spotted signs directing travelers to two different queues: "United States Citizens" and "Aliens." Even in my sleep-deprived state, I knew what the word "alien" meant. An alien is a creature from another planet—a "little green man," or one of the otherworldly critters I'd seen in *Star Wars* and other science fiction dramas I'd enjoyed while immersed in Western popular culture at China's version of Hogwarts. Now, as a young woman embarking on a new life in a new land, there were extraterrestrial beings waiting to receive me. *Wow,* I remember thinking to myself, *you really can find absolutely anything in America.*

As crowds of people from all over the globe swirled around me in the terminal, I considered the signs again. I wasn't a US citizen, so by process of elimination, I steered myself in the other direction. I picked up my suitcase, inhaled deeply, and prepared myself emotionally to meet the aliens. As I did so, I reflected on how harrowing the journey to America had been.

America Bound

When I resigned my post in Dalian in October 1989, the Chinese economy was in recession. Upon returning to Beijing, I began scouring job listings so I could make a living. In my spare time, I negotiated the intimidating Chinese bureaucracy, trying to secure a passport—an especially daunting task following the Tiananmen incident. Most Westerners could apply for a passport at a local post office, but Chinese citizens could only travel abroad under two special circumstances: work and family. If Chinese nationals had a business engagement or foreign meeting to attend, officials often issued them a passport that their bosses or managers kept to ensure that the holder returned to China. Barring business abroad, Chinese applicants had to demonstrate that a close family member lived overseas, and that they had a legitimate reason for visiting that relative.

I planned to take advantage of a major loophole in the system. If the government granted you a passport to visit a family member, you could visit any Western country for which you were granted a visa. One of my father's relatives lived in Canada, and so I applied to travel overseas to officially visit his family, but really to use the passport to pursue graduate studies in America. To secure this passport to Canada, I needed approval from no fewer than 10 official organizations, verifying my relationship with Dad's relative, and my former employer who arranged my work in Dalian, ensuring that I hadn't made any major mistakes during my tenure there.

Dealing with bureaucracy is frustrating at best, and sometimes dehumanizing. Many officials who lacked power in their lives asserted it here, sometimes denying people like me a fair shot for no reason. I'd stand in line for hours just to have an official reject my passport application because a single page supposedly lacked a comma, or some other trivial mistake. When I inquired about the precise sin I'd committed, they'd tell me to review the entire dossier. This was the analogue era, when no electronic documents existed, and no one corresponded over email. Sometimes, after a rejection like that, I'd have to return to several government organizations and bureaus to secure fresh, grammatically correct copies of my forms. Dejected after months of such maddening disapproval, I was ready to give up entirely, when a family friend gave me some curious advice: "Treat yourself like a cabbage."

You must understand Beijing to appreciate her wisdom. As cold descends on the city each winter, white cabbage is one of the only vegetables still in abundance. Because cabbages are easy to store and remain robust and vitamin-rich through the cold, urban residents purchase them in bulk, loading them onto their bicycles and stockpiling them in sheds outside their homes so they're shielded from direct sunlight and humidity. On winter days, you can easily take a cabbage inside the home, dust it off, peel away any wilted outer layers, and decide on one of myriad ways to prepare it. You might pair the vegetable with glass noodles in giant hot pots, use cabbage to bulk up a tofu stew, ferment it to make Korean-style kimchi, or—my personal favorite—mix it with pork as filling for dumplings. What my friend was trying to say was that for bureaucrats, I was just like this winter staple: extremely abundant, nonexotic, and at times, grudgingly endured. I realized that each time I'd been singled out and rejected, I'd reacted as if the slight were personal.

I took my friend's advice and thought about myself as a cabbage, depersonalizing the bureaucratic red tape. This made me a lot happier. Each time I thought of cabbages, I remembered how great they tasted in my mom's pork dumplings. And I thought about Chinese government clerks and began to empathize with them. After all, I was applying to embark on a life of possibility and plenty in America, while they would never be able to travel for work or pleasure.

The bicycle commute to these offices during Beijing's prolonged winter season also posed difficulties. I had to ensure my wheels remained in the grooves of snow left behind from the other bikers. I'd learned the hard way that if I veered away from those pre-worn tracks, my bike might collide with a snowbank, sending me and my belongings flying. I'd fallen from my bike many times this way, and the impact from the crash or from other bikes striking me from behind had left me bloody and my paperwork soaked in watery soot. For another six or seven months I endured this daily routine, until one day I'd managed to submit satisfactory paperwork.

That day, as I've recounted, I managed to fill my trusty plastic garbage bag full of years of savings. And yet the teller who had counted the money and stamped my application had granted me only a temporary victory. She'd eliminated the first obstacle, ensuring me a passport, but now I needed to apply for a visa to the United States. This process proved even more daunting than the passport. As I discovered, many elderly people spent their days outside Beijing's US Embassy, playing chess and watching people emerge from the building crying because their applications had been rejected. The elderly somehow delighted in this theater of misery. My spirits sagged at discovering this, and our driver for the World Bank and UNDP office, who liked to gossip about what he saw when delivering guests and documents at the American Embassy, didn't help. His car had diplomatic tags and he had high-security clearance, allowing him access to international news and the latest goings-on. He always smiled cheerfully at me and complimented my English—though he didn't speak a word of it himself—all the while sharing his observations. "I don't see many people coming back with a visa," he told me. "Yesterday 200 people entered, and maybe 40 got it. The day before, 250 entered, and maybe only 30."

By the time of my interview at the US Embassy, a full year had elapsed since I'd departed Dalian. It was December 1990 and, once again, extreme cold had descended on Beijing. I arrived early in the morning to beat the rush, armed with my hard-earned passport, financial statements detailing my family income, and a letter from the University of Maryland, College Park, granting me admission to a master's program in journalism for the 1991 spring semester.

The embassy official asked what I planned to study in America. "Mass communication," I replied.

"Why would you want to study that?" he asked. He was legitimately perplexed. Most Chinese students were STEM-focused, and applied to study math, chemistry, and physics in US universities. No one, especially in China, went to study a discipline called "journalism." I introduced the topic with genuine enthusiasm, explaining how my work at the World Bank had interested me in the topic, and that I was intrigued by how people across the world communicated with one another.

The diplomatic official complimented my English, and I told him that I'd had the good fortune of pursuing a university program focused on foreign studies in Beijing. The entire interview lasted no more than five minutes, and the only document in my dossier he was interested in seeing was my letter of admission from the University of Maryland. "Congratulations," he said. "You will now continue your studies in America." Many whose visa applications were declined told me how "exceptionally lucky" I had been to score an official as lenient and kind-hearted as he was.

Stranger in a Strange Land

John Kalbermatten, the World Bank veteran who'd helped me through my airplane-induced motion sickness years before, heard I'd secured my passport, US visa, and admission to graduate school. And when he learned I was moving to America without my family, he generously offered to sponsor the trip and host me. John bought me a one-way airline ticket, which probably cost $1,000 at the time, and he also insisted I stay with him and his wife in Washington, DC, so I could take my time to find suitable accommodations of my own.

After making my way through the alien line, I found John and his wife, Nelly, both in their late sixties, waiting for me in the Dulles international terminal. We drove to their residence, located at the corner of Wisconsin and Massachusetts avenues, near all the foreign embassies in the US capital as well as the magnificent National Cathedral and Navy Observatory. I'd never been to a stand-alone home, with no neighbors above, below, or bordering me on either side, and I'd never seen unoccupied surplus bedrooms and large common areas. It was such a stark difference from the small, dark homes in China that it induced immediate culture shock.

John and Nelly's three grown children had long since departed their family home, and I was given a room formerly occupied by Leslie, the youngest child, who in her youth had enjoyed a round princess mattress. As they explained, the house had central air conditioning and heating, which I could adjust for my comfort, and my room came equipped with its own television that I could program with a remote control. As I lay there in bed that night, warm and happy, I felt like a princess in an exotic land; I didn't want to succumb to the jet lag and sleep, just so I could enjoy it more. Perhaps most intoxicating of all was the peace and solitude in the house, unlike anything I'd experienced growing up in China. The wall-to-wall carpeting elegantly absorbed all ambient noise and before long I was fast asleep, dreaming of little green aliens.

In the months that followed, I basked in my new city. Washington, DC, was beautiful—residential lawns were green even in the winter, not gray and yellowish like the vegetation dotting China in the colder months. As winter yielded to spring, cherry blossoms and tulips sprouted throughout the city. The green color and cleanliness mesmerized me. So, too, did the city's classical architecture. It gave me such pleasure to see the tasteful bungalows and Craftsman-style homes, to gradually distinguish them from the more ornate Tudor and Victorian dwellings, and to glimpse the occasional contemporary home, with large picture windows, straight lines, and open-concept rooms. Gothic, Greek, and Georgian diplomatic buildings, lined with flags from the world over, distinguished embassy row near John and Nelly's home, giving me a special thrill, reminiscent as they were of my passion for diplomacy.

The Atlantic seaboard's urban landscape was such a contrast to China, where multistory, utilitarian condominiums of cement and brick lined the residential boulevards, all built to accommodate the throngs of people moving from the countryside to the city. While Hangzhou was beautiful in the spring, the sheer number of people in China meant that everything was always crowded. In Washington, green space dominated, with children peacefully playing, enjoying beautiful, spacious homes and yards.

John and Nelly were extremely gracious hosts, introducing me to different parts of the city and to new phases of the American experience. They made my transition to graduate studies a lot easier. The University of Maryland, I discovered after beginning class a few weeks after I arrived, had all the charming qualities of a quaint American campus, with red-brick Georgian buildings, abundant stretches of lawn, and a diverse, multicultural student body. My English was so strong that, unlike many other Asian immigrants and foreign nationals, no one on campus struggled to understand me.

The *Washington Post*, *Wall Street Journal*, and *New York Times* became my school textbooks, as each day my journalism professors required us to read all the major dailies to develop an intimate understanding of current events. The precise value of the national debt, the name and hometown of the US soldier felled by friendly fire in the American engagement in Iraq, the climate of censorship in the Soviet Union—our instructors ensured we knew it all and could make impromptu presentations on each topic. For the first time since boarding school, I found myself scrambling to keep up with the reading, writing, and subject matter. Though China had continued to open itself up to Western influences, especially since my youth in the Cultural Revolution, I was also moving from a state-controlled media environment that presented highly ideological documentaries and news reports to an open Western media landscape. Whether they were praising or criticizing, journalists spoke so openly about the government that it was shocking.

I graduated with my journalism degree in December 1992, just in time for the economic downturn that was convulsing the American economy. As is the case in many developed countries, foreign students in America aren't allowed to pursue employment opportunities off campus. This was unfortunate, since many journalism graduate students complemented their studies with internships that afforded them a year or two of practical job training. My immigration status posed another problem. Though I had a journalism degree focused on mass communication and was qualified for many industry jobs, most available posts were policy or government related and required a green card or US passport. Journalism has never been an especially lucrative calling, but the Internet revolution has created a proliferation of media outlets and opportunities for freelance work. In the analogue environment of the mid-1990s, however, such employment offerings were scarce. If I couldn't find a job, I'd have to return to China.

Thankfully, in January 1993, I secured a position in New York City at a company called the US-China Industrial Exchange. My new employer's history and mission inspired me. Two young American women had struck up a friendship while studying Chinese at Columbia University, and they both decided to move to China and start a business after graduation. This was a rare decision in the late 1980s, especially for two females in their early twenties. The two rented a hotel room in Beijing and started what would become one of the first medical equipment export companies incorporated in America but operating in China. This unique value proposition soon made the company successful, as they found a broad Chinese market interested in purchasing GE's computerized tomography (CT) and magnetic resonance imaging (MRI) machines, Acuson's ultrasound technologies, and Spacelab's hospital beds.

As grateful as I was for this job, I can't say my first work experience in the United States was a satisfying one. As the assistant export manager, I occupied a low-end, paper-pushing office role, ensuring that most of the company's import–export banking loan and medical equipment information was filed with the government in perfect English and on time. In addition to reams of paperwork, I'd spend weekends and evenings receiving buyers from Chinese hospitals who were visiting American factories and evaluating medical equipment— all for an annual salary of $19,000, significantly less than I'd made working part-time in China. I also suffered thanks to my new job's location. David's training in physics and his background in seismology and marine science landed him a position working for a navy contractor in Washington, DC. When I agreed to this job in New York, I also agreed to a long weekly commute. For a year and a half, I'd live in New York during the week and return home to Greenbelt, Maryland, on the weekends.

The job slowly ground me down. As in Dalian, I sensed that my potential wasn't being realized and that I wasn't adding value to the company. My immediate supervisor was mean-spirited, approaching my desk around 4:30 each afternoon to tell me all the mistakes I'd made that day, ensuring I'd stay late into the night to correct them. Strong-arming me was the only tactic she knew to establish her authority and demonstrate her worthiness for a promotion. Knowing I was for-eigner on a practical training visa with limited job options, she often volunteered me to do extra translation work or to retrieve a traveling junket of Chinese doctors over the weekend and take them sightseeing around New York.

This behavior went unchecked because the company's two founders, whom I admired, worked in Beijing and exercised little control over the culture at the New York office. As a conflict-avoidant second child who came of age in a culture that strongly discouraged personal confrontations, I struggled with setting personal boundaries. But even if I'd been prepared to respond more forcefully, my options were limited. After this experience, I vowed I would never work for a boss again, and I would show any future employees of mine the appreciation they deserved.

My loneliness in New York was such a contrast to the celebrity treatment I'd enjoyed with John and Nelly after first landing in Washington. Without friends or disposable income, I retreated every day to my small room. The bustling and rich city swirling around me only compounded my feeling of isolation, reminding me that I was in the midst of a wonderful world and yet I was entirely outside of it. I had the freedom to cook, but I barely earned enough to purchase quality ingredients. After a day of defeat at work, I had no energy to explore the museums, galleries, or other cultural treasures of the big city, like I had while in college in Beijing.

Winters were the worst. I think my mom's reeducation in the north of China and my own experience in Dalian led me to associate frigid temperatures and snow with dread and hopelessness. In New York, I had to wait for buses in the snow. Sometimes, if I was late, I'd run to catch the bus only to see it disappear into the gray morning, leaving me to wait an hour for another one. It wasn't the driver's fault; even if he could see me running, he still had to stay on schedule. But I couldn't help but personalize the situation, believing that New York in general was anti-Mei.

David was a pillar of strength during this time. When I returned home on the weekends and cried on his shoulder, he reminded me to focus on the positive parts of our lives and to remember that this job wouldn't last forever. As a rational, scientific type, he was calmer than I was and helped tame the more temperamental and emotional aspects of my nature. But there was only so much solace he could provide. Because he inhabited a world of formulas and data, he never understood how diminishing it was for people focused on ideas and relationships to receive only negative feedback from a peer or boss. He also now occupied a post worthy of his talents and background, while I felt underutilized.

In fact, I suffered the opposite problem. As a highly adaptable person who immediately took to American language and culture, I thrived on social contact and would have excelled in the marketing or strategy departments of my medical device company. Unlike my introverted husband, I could have expanded the company in new directions, using my social skills to find new vendors and cement new alliances. But the company considered me its charity case—the Mandarin speaker needed to perform basic secretarial work. As I've observed over my career, middle managers the world over seem more intent on hiring people whom they can control rather than finding bright and promising people and empowering them to flourish. Later on, when I owned my own company, I'd always try to coach my middle managers out of this mentality, telling them, "I know there is a truism that A-level talent hires B-level talent, and B-level talent in turn finds C-level. I expect the opposite from you—there's room for everyone to succeed." We need top talent throughout the organization, I always advised, and there's room for everyone to have a good job.

Despite the indignity and hardship, New York granted me one indulgence. During those lonely days and evenings, I'd venture to Bloomingdale's and bask in its treasures. I allowed the ladies with perfume bottles to spray my wrists and I delighted in getting lost in the aisles, among the racks of colorful women's fashion. For one of the first times in my life, I encountered fashion items in an intimate, sensory way. Bloomingdale's represented the much-vaunted American Dream, a place to shop after you'd really made it. I couldn't afford anything I saw, and that hardly mattered—the store's very existence represented a glimmer of hope that this dream might be accessible to others, even underpaid immigrants like me. The presence of so many items arranged with such care unleashed my pent-up and stifled creative energies. It reactivated my interest in fashion and design, something I'd possessed since elementary school, defiantly wearing pedal pushers and blue jeans. In China, there was no opportunity to study fashion, much less appreciate it, since everyone wore the same clothes. Here, people of means could adorn themselves with an endless variety of glamorous options.

But something else struck me as I wandered around Bloomie's. There was a marked contrast between the bright, bold color patterns in the clothing department and the rather plain and drab offerings in home goods, located a few floors away. In fact, the department store's houseware offerings, featuring dreary beige curtains, cherrywood stools, and flowered wallpaper, reminded me of pictures I'd seen in textbooks of American homes during the Great Depression or the conformity-driven 1950s. They were heavy, lifeless, and boring, lacking any burst of color or seasonal variation. The home furnishings on offer in this world-class department store unmistakably screamed in both Mandarin and English, "Grandma!"

This discrepancy gnawed at me. Surely, I thought, there must be a way to bring the modern and fresh style of American fashion into home furnishing and décor. This idea eventually transformed into a dream, one that would loom large as I imagined my future: the world needed not another fashion designer. It needed a designer to help create a fashionable home.

Pacific Traders

As I languished away in New York, I'd hardly noticed that macroeconomic and geopolitical trends were pointing toward a home interiors revolution. The world was undergoing a major transition, becoming increasingly interconnected, globalized, and culturally enmeshed. Not only could people travel more easily to exotic locations around the globe, but Western companies like Nike and Calvin Klein ventured abroad as well, traveling to Asia in search of cheaper labor markets and aesthetic inspiration. Fashion was becoming a global cultural expression as major retailers and designers drew on the world's richness to create and launch their collections in new and diverse markets.

Many of my Chinese friends began noticing these trends, and instead of seeking diplomatic posts, began pursuing global business opportunities, especially ones involving trade between China and the United States. I performed preliminary market research and discovered that Chinese companies had competitive labor markets and industrial facilities capable of manufacturing anything from bed linens to furniture to decorative lighting. Dissatisfied with our current jobs, David and I delved deeper into these trends and evaluated our options. The economic recession and my visa status left me ineligible for broadcasting and public affairs jobs, while David's gainful employment as a government contractor left him socially isolated and restless. He longed to work in an entrepreneurial setting, as he had during and after college, thinking about startups, seeding new ventures, and following the latest technology and market trends, all of which energized him and allowed his natural personality and charisma to shine. We looked for niche markets we might enter and noticed that while hard commodities and fashion were extremely competitive, gaps existed in home-based

Chinese exports. One day, we spontaneously said to each other, "Let's try our hand at the import business and test some home products."

In April 1994, we quit our jobs, I relocated from New York to Maryland, and we embarked on a new life as business owners. It was a scary leap, born of desperation and our longing for a new and better life. Our expenses were modest—we rented a $500 apartment, lived frugally, and had amassed a modest savings of $30,000 thanks to David's job. That summer, we traveled to China and explored the diversity of products manufactured there, considering which ones might resonate among Americans. In August, we returned to Maryland armed with samples of window curtains, silk flowers, music dolls, Chinese paper fans with elaborate decorations, car cushions—and a few decorative candles.

We didn't understand the seasonal retail calendar and our timing was unfortunate. As we'd later learn, the big, wholesale-focused trade shows usually happen from June to August. Small mom-and-pop stores place their holiday orders in time for products to be manufactured, shipped, and received by October, well ahead of the Christmas holiday season. By September, when we arrived with our product samples, many merchants had already filled their inventories from the big Atlanta and New York gift shows earlier that summer. But as we gathered our samples and conducted additional research, we saw that one gift show in Charlotte, North Carolina, was still a few weeks out. Knowing that if we didn't attend, we'd have to wait until the following January to begin, we purchased a 10x10-foot booth and decided to make this show our inaugural venture, offering our wares and testing the US consumer market. David and I drew on our personal savings and borrowed from parents and friends to purchase our inventory and launch our fledgling enterprise.

We called ourselves Pacific Trade International—not the cleverest name, but one that connoted China and foreign interchange. We rented an office space in Laurel, Maryland, with a showroom in front and a two-thousand-square-foot warehouse in back. Although we were new to the consumer products space, we weren't naïve and never wanted to resemble what in China is known as "the briefcase guy": a salesperson without an office, samples, or warehouse who instead hocks ideas and concepts from a fashionable bag. David had enough entrepreneurial experience to know that we couldn't experiment with the market as a briefcase operation. I worked as the secretary, accountant, salesperson, and warehouse point person, and we hired our first assistant, a college student from the University of Maryland, who worked after school.

In September 1994, we loaded our samples into a rented van and headed south. After driving for more than six hours, we collided with a truck while making a left turn. Though we emerged unscathed, I couldn't help but get a sinking feeling, imagining it an inauspicious beginning to our new business. Nevertheless, we made it to Charlotte, North Carolina, unloaded the contents of our damaged van, arranged our samples in our booth, and, miraculously, attracted consumer interest. Hospital gift stores and mom-and-pop stores from Florida, Atlanta, and other southern states sifted through our 10 different product categories, but all seemed to gravitate to only one item: the glow candles.

Mei debuts magic glow candles and other products from China at the Charlotte Gift Show (1994).

David and I scratched our heads as we returned to our hotel room that evening, pondering why 60 to 70 percent of our orders were candles. We could never have guessed that this product would emerge victorious. It was the smallest item and for that reason alone seemed to lack potential—it wasn't especially eye-catching. China had no domestic candle industry, and I'd never grown up with the idea of using candles to add a special illumination or intimate feel to our evening spaces. In my youth, candles were utilitarian objects, dusted off when the electricity unexpectedly failed and we needed to light our homes. They were also ceremonial and religious objects, with red taper candles glowing outside the Buddhist temple complexes of my native Hangzhou.

Over the course of this four-day fair, candles appeared on almost every retail store order form we received, proving that these emergency or religious items from my youth now enjoyed a broader consumer appeal in America. Thrilled at the candles' surprising popularity, we could hardly sleep at night and started each day eager to speak with more customers. After the show closed each evening, we rushed back to our hotel room and faxed the day's candle orders to our assistant in Maryland so that she could ship them right away. The faster she worked, the quicker the stores could sell the inventory and reorder.

During the early 1990s, Amazon's superstore didn't yet dominate retail. Instead, unique, mom-and-pop retailers flourished in cities and suburban strip malls, along with classic department stories like Macy's and JC Penney that advertised their products in glossy, high-end catalogs. Prior to migrating online and becoming more centralized, retail was personal, and the small shop owners with whom we spoke served specific market niches and had deep knowledge of consumer product preferences and larger retail and industry trends. We couldn't wait to speak to these fellow small business owners and discuss current trends, and we also loved seeing them lean into our display, fascinated by the way the flames illuminated the designs emblazoned on the outside of the round candles.

David gravitated to technical matters and specialized in answering granular questions about the life and longevity of candles, while also tabulating our sales and inventory numbers and staying up late to phone in or fax our numbers to China. His polite mannerisms and attentiveness also endeared him to our customers, especially the older ones, who loved that such a handsome man was eager to engage with them. David could finally shine again in a social and business setting. For the first time in a while, I too encountered productive and satisfying challenges. I began mastering different regional accents and dialects from America's South and Midwest regions, reading body language like I had at the World Bank and learning how to balance small talk and personable engagement while still seizing every opportunity to close a deal.

As it turned out, many of our first customers reordered within weeks of receiving their shipments, powering the momentum of our young startup. During our initial four months of business, beginning in the fall of 1994, we worked overtime to ensure our customers were happy and that their inventory was plentiful. After meeting us at that first show, Kirkland's, a Tennessee-based chain store with around 300 locations, ordered around $100,000 worth of candles that fall and holiday ("Falliday") season. Looking back, I'm shocked that we generated such interest and were able to deliver such a massive order in our first year. Such success was unprecedented, especially for people lacking business training, marketing know-how, and investment. For most small vendors like us, it took 10 to 15 years to generate the profits that David and I experienced from just testing the market.

Having notched over $500,000 worth of orders by the end of 1994, we were officially profitable. Feeling competent and professionally energized for the first time in years, David and I invited both of our staff members to a celebration at a local Chinese restaurant. This karaoke-themed dinner began a 20-year tradition in which our staff convened to mark important company milestones or holidays like Chinese New Year. Often, we hosted company potlucks, asking each staff member to bring a favorite dish to share with the group.

To continue our celebration, David and I flew to Florida to visit Disney World over the Christmas holiday. This might seem like an odd choice for a couple with no children, but as new immigrants we really wanted to explore this iconic piece of Americana. Besides, we didn't have family around and loved the idea of escaping the drabness of winter for Florida. But after Christmas, we were equally excited about returning to work and beginning to prepare for the year's major trade shows.

In January 1995, David and I attended the Chicago Gift Show, located in McCormick Place. We rented a $40 room at a suburban Red Roof Inn and on opening day waited 45 minutes in the brutal cold for the downtown-bound shuttle to retrieve us. Our festival booth was situated next to an exit door and even with gloves on we could barely keep our fingers warm enough to grasp our items and hold them steady on the shelf as gusts of wintry wind blew through.

As I struggled in the cold, I experienced a moment of sadness and creeping doubt. "What an incredibly hard way to earn a living," I thought. We couldn't enjoy our success or afford to take a salary,

I further reasoned, as we had to reinvest any profits into more inventory. But such self-pity didn't last. The moment people began filing into our booth I became energized, mixing and mingling with my customers and vendors with boundless energy. Any misgivings I had were overcome by our rapidly expanding customer base, which by the end of that show comprised about 600 mom-and-pop retailers throughout the country and 2–3 larger department stores.

We were on a high as we left Chicago and prepared for the "Super-bowl" of American wholesale events: the New York International Gift Fair. As it turned out, we would come away from Manhattan's Jacob Javits Center the following month stunned and disappointed. No one seemed interested in our products and no one stopped to ask questions. "Oh, this looks great for Christmas," a few people said, implying that now, in the post-holiday retail season, our product was passé. At previous shows I had kept busy writing orders and speaking to people, but this time I had little to do, so I wandered around surveying the oceans of booths. I had never seen so many diverse products in my life. About 50 different companies, for example, offered decorative pillows, some with intricate Indian designs that reminded me of henna tattoos, others that were text-driven or conversational in style, with words like MOM emblazoned in neutral tones.

To my dismay, some 200 booths offered different arrays of candles. They all had a similar appearance, with jar containers and dull colors, but they all came fragranced. I paused. While I'd always assumed that consumers purchased candles because they were beautiful, I could now see that scent appealed to them as well. It made sense: a home-maker might finish cleaning a home and burn a candle as a ceremonial gesture, giving the newly clean place a fresh scent and a warm, relaxing feel. Candles, I realized, were affordable luxuries. In failing to visit retail stores that post-holiday season, I hadn't understood this, and as a result I'd treated candles as purely decorative items instead of functional ones that elevated one's mood, status, and energy.

Realizing that I'd overlooked something powerful about my product, I felt energized and was determined to correct this mistake. I'd look for clues about how to improve my product design later that month in Europe while attending Ambiente, the grande dame of global trade shows that takes place each winter in Frankfurt, Germany. While most trade shows were gift-oriented, this one was industrial in focus and included home furnishings, interior design, and kitchen appliances and gadgetry galore. Still bootstrapping entrepreneurs, we deplaned from our Dulles to Frankfurt red-eye flight and, in bleary-eyed exhaustion, headed to a cheap hotel we'd selected near the central Frankfurt train station.

"How many hours do you want?" the attendant asked.

We changed course immediately and sought out a room closer to the city center. We couldn't afford the hotels that the trade show recommended in its programming materials, but we could do better than a rent-by-the-hour brothel.

It was the dead of winter in Germany, but the trade show was lively, bright, and colorful. I walked the aisles, immersing myself in the endless offerings of sofas, coffee machines, and dinnerware. I noticed handmade ceramics and compared the shiny glaze of some products with the matte finish of others. Next, I scanned the wide variety of glasses, some with stone finishes and others complete with an acid wash. Furniture makers experimented with organic touches and textures, the presence of natural wood tones and the absence of paint endowing their pieces with a sense of harmony and nature. Unlike the New York trade show, which still featured the traditional color schemes I'd seen in Bloomingdale's, the European color palette was bold, vivid, and edgy, pairing bright yellows and oranges with crisp navy blues and lavenders. Everything appeared sharper, elevated, elegant, and clean.

Whether the medium was glass, wood, or ceramic, and whether the items were large home furnishings or simple throw pillows, texture and expressions of individuality prevailed. The Europeans had translated the fashions of Donna Karen and Calvin Klein into home décor. The longing that I had experienced in Bloomingdale's had finally materialized. But this sensibility hadn't yet migrated to candles. I saw a few wrought-iron and copper candle holders, carved to look like twisted tree trunks and finished with a dark cast, but the creativity ended there. In Europe, either votives or tapers—those long skinny candles you burn at the dinner table—remained in vogue, and they seemed to disappear against the backdrop of these bolder home furnishings, still lacking fragrances and retaining a dull and lifeless color palette.

Aesthetically, European candle manufacturers were much like the large American candle companies, showing an affinity for hunter green, mulberry, and bland navy, the color palette of "Grandma's village." I don't mean to disparage or insult this look; such country-style design certainly had market appeal. But as a native of China, I had no familiarity or nostalgia for country style and instead gravitated to contemporary design, with artist-white backgrounds and bold, fresh, energetic colors. I could almost smell the fragrance I wanted them to emit, and for the first time I began thinking in an olfactory way.

My vision of more contemporary home décor—doing for candles what the fashion industry had done for textiles and what Europeans had done for home furnishings—almost seemed within grasp. In Frankfurt, I'd stumbled upon the aesthetic I wanted to capture and convey. I was now convinced that the future of our business rested on creating contemporary candle offerings based on a refreshing and invigorating set of fragrances, bold color palettes, and fresh and crisp labels.

But our biggest innovation had to be design-based. I disliked the mass-produced shiny taper candles that had a plastic-like finish. Instead, I wanted to apply a texture to the candle that I'd seen in the contemporary decorative pieces on offer in Germany. I wanted to somehow capture the luxury and refinement that these contemporary European home furnishings epitomized. If I'd studied fashion, I'd have understood that ultimate luxury resides in the marriage of texture and color. Lacking this background, I instead let my intuition lead me, gravitating to the smooth and radiant silk and soft-linen textures that had enchanted me as a child and now spoke to me in adulthood. I was overcome with emotion that day, almost tearing up. I'd found my market niche and my larger life calling.

A Happy Accident

It was early 1996, and as I imagined the transformation of our products, our glow-candle company was growing. We moved our base of operations to a large industrial park in Upper Marlboro, Maryland, with a bigger warehouse and office space to accommodate a larger inventory and staff. During my real estate search that year, I found a modest home in Crownsville, Maryland. Its remote location made it affordable, and its unfinished basement provided me a perfect place to experiment with candles.

We began hiring representatives to knock on doors and forge relationships, introducing people to the charm of the glow candle. I

Richard Zhu in the Upper Marlboro, Maryland, office (1996).

hired a sales manager, Sharon Walsh, a chain-smoker and veteran jewelry industry worker from New York, who proved indispensable at filling our orders, along with David's friend, Richard Zhu. The son of two elite science professors in Beijing, Richard grew up during the Cultural Revolution like us, struggling to acquire an education when the country exiled its professional classes to learn from peasants in the countryside. Because his formal schooling was so poor, Richard watched a grainy black-and-white dormitory television, picking up enough English and basic math skills from the educational offerings to test into an elite private school like me. After college he worked at the mechanical engineering company Dapoly, where he made about six or seven times as much as his college professor parents did and where he met David.

Later, after stints at an American medical device company and at IBM, Richard accepted an invitation to join our glow-candle company and live with us in our small home outside Chesapeake Bay. During his more than 20-year tenure with the company, Richard served a variety of roles, initially helping us with order processing, warehouse management, packing and shipping, accounts receivable, money collection, and payment processing. He even unpacked pallets of product and drove the forklift around the warehouse. We worked late nights together, shared meals, and ventured to local malls on the weekends looking for new candle products and home-fashion items to stay abreast of consumer trends. He eventually led operations and helped grow our company from a small glow-candle purveyor to a design-driven industry leader.

Around the time Richard came on board, I began dreaming about colors and fragrances and creating my own apprenticeships and research opportunities to familiarize myself with these industries. There's no university degree or vocational program that teaches candle-making, let alone how to procure colors or infuse wax with fragrances. Many industries in America lack this basic infrastructure and training, especially since we've exported manufacturing abroad. My Chinese upbringing didn't provide much help—the country lacked a native fragrance industry, exporting ingredients like cinnamon, sandalwood, and jasmine flowers but never compounding them domestically.

Though the Egyptians, Persians, and Arabs had developed ointments and balms, the modern fragrance industry got its start in the lavender fields and rosebushes of southern France, where chemists captured these native aromas and applied them to foodstuffs and toiletries alike. The world's best purveyors of fragrance are usually renowned for gastronomy, too, because taste and fragrance are inherent companions, enhancing the natural flavors of food and improving human hygiene and self-presentation, especially in eras without modern plumbing.

When I returned home from Frankfurt, I asked my customers for a fragrance instructor. Several mentioned Peter French, the founder of French Color & Fragrance Co., who would become my fragrance guru. One day in spring 1996, Richard and I piled into his beat-up hatchback and drove to Peter's laboratory in New Jersey, located just beyond the George Washington Bridge. A delightful man in his early sixties at the time, Peter gave us an expert overview of the art and science of candle-coloring and fragrance-infusion. Candle wax, we learned, melts at relatively low temperatures (99° Fahrenheit). That melting point is the sweet spot, the moment to incorporate dyes and oils or to take advantage of wax's extraordinary plasticity to fashion Christmas trees, Easter eggs, or cylindrical birthday-candle shapes. Peter taught us about UV protection and how to blend colors and fragrances evenly, avoiding large color clumps or the premature graying of wax and enabling the aroma to emit evenly for the duration of the candle's lifecycle. We left Peter's laboratory that day armed with knowledge and 10 fragrance and dye samples. I only purchased scents and colors that aligned with my larger color palette and fragrance vision, avoiding hunter greens, dull navies, and anything that suggested the color or taste of berries.

At home with my goodies, I noticed that the candle molds I'd ordered hadn't yet arrived, so I scoured my home for suitable wax receptacles. I settled on some Campbell's soup cans that I had cleaned, dried, and placed in the kitchen recycling bin. I ferried these empty cans downstairs and set them next to the electric stove and big metal pots I'd purchased for my experiments. Just as Peter had instructed, I began melting the wax and blending oils and colors, combining the lavender color and fragrance into one can, pairing French vanilla with a soft white color in another, fresh honeydew fragrance with a limey green color, a sunflower fragrance with bright yellow, and then putting a bold orange scent and color together.

When I awoke the next morning and eagerly ventured downstairs to survey the experiments, I gasped. I'd committed a major error, forgetting to use vybar, a chemical ingredient that allows for the even blending of colors and fragrance oils and for the wax's marbleized, consistent finish. Absent the vybar, my blending was uneven, yielding a series of odd ephemeral snowflakes coating each candle. But what a happy accident, as this was exactly the unique texture I'd dreamed about!

If I'd never ventured to the Germany trade show and imagined the future of candle-making, I'd probably have lacked the confidence to proceed with this error and would have retried the experiment, this time incorporating vybar. But my vision was firmly in place, as was my understanding of cutting-edge consumer tastes and where they might steer the market. This was, I thought, the textural and aesthetic change that just might revolutionize candle-making.

That morning, as I performed victory cartwheels across the basement, I couldn't have known where these candles would ultimately lead me. But I knew I could capitalize on the flourishing Chinese-America trade relationship to bring the excitement, patterns, and colors from fashion to the specific niche of home furnishings. And having taken that vision and created a business around it, I had arrived at a new understanding of myself. I'd always seemed dogged by bad luck—destined for defeat. I was a great student, but each time I graduated, I seemed to encounter some major obstacle, resulting in unfulfilling or exploitative working arrangements. But now it hit me: Mei, a timid, second child, who'd always existed in the larger shadows of others, had done the riskiest and boldest thing imaginable. She'd started a business.

First Chesapeake Bay pillar candle ever made, in the basement of Mei's home (1996).

It was, I should add, a business that we could only have hatched in America. Chinese culture values stable and prestigious jobs, like government, university, or research posts, and many would have viewed starting a business in a "trivial" consumer good as undignified. Throughout the world, but especially in China, a longstanding stigma exists against the so-called merchant trades. Little did I know that all my training in foreign language and diplomacy would be indispensable as I came to grapple with global retail markets, the dynamism of international supply chains, and heated negotiations with some of the country's biggest retailers. I was certainly naïve at this moment, thinking that I could easily telegraph my aesthetic visions onto different candle canvases, work with factories overseas that could realize these visions, and manufacture and ship these products to the United States, where I could distribute them to a diversity of retailers. I had no idea about all of the material and geopolitical obstacles that stood in my path. And that's probably for the best. All I saw was possibility and opportunity.

America had provided me with the entrepreneurial ecosystem to conceive of an idea, test it in the market, and achieve success. It's no wonder that so many immigrants come to America and become entrepreneurs. There's something about the spirit of entrepreneurs and immigrants alike, a preternatural optimism that smolders like a candle, guiding us to transcend our humble or unfortunate circumstances, take risks, and achieve. Somehow, that's exactly what I'd done. I'd landed at Dulles airport as an alien, and five years later, I was close to achieving the American Dream.

- Timing is important in business. By sheer luck, David and I timed our entry to the market in the mid-1990s, during the US–Sino honeymoon period of economic relations.
- Hard work is even more important in business. I never stopped testing the market, evaluating my products and refining my designs based on retail customer and consumer feedback, as well as experiences at global trade shows.
- If you are an immigrant, resist the urge to completely assimilate and instead hold fast to your rich cultural background, leveraging it to detect cultural trends and discover market gaps that you can fill.
- If you are a native-born American, adopt an immigrant's perspective.
- I created a design-focused business lacking any formal education and training in this field, relying on my lifelong passion for art and my unique ability to spot cultural and fashion trends. What are you uniquely positioned to create?

3

AMERICAN ENTREPRENEURS

Despite its charming docks, beautiful vistas, and great summer sunsets, Chesapeake Bay had a mixed reputation when I arrived in the United States in the early 1990s. Most Americans only considered it serene and peaceful from a distance. Deforestation, overfishing, and industrial runoff in the mid-Atlantic region had exacted a devastating environmental toll, decreasing the bay's once-abundant oyster harvests and fish yields and compromising the enjoyment of the place for boaters, kayakers, and frolicking children alike.

In mid-1996, when I began walking the bay's shores and studying its topography, I fell in love with the natural beauty. On spring days, I enjoyed watching the wind fill the triangular sails of the skipjack boats, powering their V-shaped hulls over the water as they dredged oysters. On the weekends, I delighted in watching recreational sailors manning a variety of different watercraft, wearing shoes that resembled tan lace-up slippers, perhaps fishing for rockfish or blue crabs, or simply indulging in the gentle ripples their boats created on the bay's glassy surface.

Chesapeake Bay supplied something I'd always craved, but had trouble finding in China: peace that arises from immersion in nature. Chinese parks and recreational spaces feature ornately planted trees and flowers, pavilions, pagodas, and manufactured islands. Besides a few bridges and tunnels, Chesapeake Bay has remained largely untouched for centuries, giving it a less contrived and even wild feel. The towns and cottages that bordered the bay's shores gave off a relaxed, historic, and easygoing vibe. The entire estuary ecosystem was *quaint*. China has picturesque places of scenic beauty—like Hangzhou's West Lake district—but with its 1.2 billion inhabitants, it had rarely offered me quaintness. In China, we loved to escape our cramped apartments and venture outside, leaving lake benches permanently occupied, outdoor attractions with hour-long wait times, and mountain and park trails teeming with humanity.

Chesapeake Bay's intimate and uncluttered surroundings allowed me to withdraw, contemplate, and reflect. And unlike Miami Beach or New York, Chesapeake Bay wasn't a famous destination and didn't have a global image to safeguard. Because it was historical without being iconic, the place suggested possibility—it was, I felt, a forgiving place that allowed for experimentation. For these reasons, the bay became my personal oasis and artistic canvas, a place where I could conjure beautiful essences, textures, scents, and even a new brand identity for my company.

One gorgeous spring day in 1996, as I walked my spirited German shepherd, named Shell, I glimpsed a cluster of plain white sails against the bay's dark blue waters, and a vision for my new candle company crystallized. My new company, featuring vybar-less candles, with their distinctive textures, fragrances, and modern color palettes, would be christened Chesapeake Bay. This name was an homage to this priceless piece of East Coast Americana. Its beautiful shores and quaint landscapes had nurtured a young republic and beckoned this recent immigrant, giving me my first experience of natural beauty and inspiring my design vision. Little did I know, this decision would anchor me in Maryland for the next three decades and determine the location of my future factory.

I also visualized a new candle label that would form a tapestry-like band around the candles. It would have an understated simplicity evoking the refreshing spring day I was experiencing, as well as the crisp colors and mild botanical fragrances of azalea and rhododendron gently washing over me. Just like Chesapeake's spring waters, I wanted my brand to evoke simplicity, elegance, and authenticity. I'd gravitated to this aesthetic my entire life, preferring simple, solid colors over flowery and frilly ones as a young girl, and then using expert tailoring to evoke sophisticated elegance when I was a cash-strapped adolescent. Now, I wished to express this aesthetic in consumer products with outdoorsy, translucent, and mottled finishes, just like the bay's springtime waters, instead of the glossy, plastic-like finishes that dominated the candle market of the time. Now, following my Campbell's soup experiments, this home décor style—which I'd first seen embodied in different media at the 1994 Frankfurt Ambiente trade show—made an appearance in the medium of wax. With the assistance of nature, I'd finally captured this aesthetic in my new brand and could convey it with my logo. On this fateful spring day, my new brand vision finally came into focus.

From Traders to Taste Makers

In May 1996, just prior to the launch of our new candle samples, we needed this new brand identity. David and I had been merchants who functioned as middlemen in the market. But following my basement candle experiments, I'd created a unique product with distinctive colors, fragrances, and textures. We now needed a brand to match these new products, one with a distinctive and bold point of view.

As a design-forward brand, Chesapeake Bay diverged from many of its Chinese counterparts. When China accelerated its exports abroad in the 1990s, its products were widely considered cheap. A "Made in China" label often signaled something low-cost and derivative at best, or bad and harmful at worst.

From the outset, Chesapeake Bay bucked the "tchotchke" reputation of Chinese products, introducing home décor items of elegance and refinement. To signal this market niche to consumers, I focused on creating brand assets by working with elements like fonts, a long-standing interest of mine that owes to my Chinese upbringing. As I've described, the Chinese Communist Party of my childhood elevated the basic, utilitarian skillsets of farmers and workers while denouncing artists, writers, musicians, and painters as bourgeois. Like many totalitarian rulers, Chairman Mao believed that the more people cultivated independent, intellectual thoughts, the more they'd threaten his power. Artistic hobbies, like painting and playing piano, were suspect.

Despite this ideological opposition to self-expression, the government allowed the long-storied art of Chinese calligraphy to continue and even flourish. In addition to being difficult to master, the calligraphic arts were always admired throughout China, and they even served as a proxy for educational attainment and a sign of virtue that could seal your fate and fortune. The art requires balance and patience because you must be willing to hold the top of a bamboo stick, affixed with a soft cosmetic-like brush, fill it with black ink, and painstakingly shape complex characters. For many, it was also a self-care activity, akin to modern-day meditation or yoga.

I was never a great practitioner of calligraphy, but my sister and father were, and they gave me a lifelong appreciation for the art and the nuances that subtle brushstrokes could convey. When I came to the United States, I noted the broad selection of available fonts in fashion magazines, newspapers, books, and product packaging, perceiving them as akin to the myriad styles of calligraphy I'd grown up with. For me, font selection was a question of artistic expression and design—something that other home décor companies underplayed.

I journeyed through various font phases, initially gravitating to Times New Roman, that giant of the serif typeface that contains strokes (serifs) on the bottom of uppercase letters (it reminded me of the "Kai Shu," or standard script of everyday Chinese calligraphy). After cementing Chesapeake Bay's new identity that summer, I developed a fascination with Century Gothic. Belonging to the sans-serif family, referring to fonts that lack extraneous strokes and frills, Century Gothic's bold geometric prints spoke to me and my new brand, and it graced nearly all of my labels during the late 1990s. Simultaneously minimalist and high impact, it elevated my design without detracting from other elements of the label, like the color and texture of the paper.

Later that May in 1996, when I traveled to a small town outside of my native Hangzhou, I realized that not everyone would welcome the understated elegance of my new brand. I'd scheduled this visit to introduce a large Chinese candle manufacturer to the new Chesapeake Bay product and gauge its interest in a partnership. The managers and sales representatives held my candle samples in their hands and frowned. My inconsistent, snowflake-like finish posed an immediate problem for them, and one of the managers gruffly complained, "This candle has too many snowflakes. That one doesn't have enough!"

"It's a random harvest," I replied.

His feedback was reasonable. Most mainstream candles included vybar because this rendered products consistent and therefore suitable for mass production and healthy profit margins. My new candles, by contrast, resembled unique pieces of art. Like nature itself, they were inconsistent and variable.

This Chinese manufacturing company was equally dubious about my fragrance infusions. I explained how Peter French compounded my unique set of scents in his New Jersey laboratory.

"Absolutely not," a representative replied. "We're not going to buy fragrances from the United States, put them in something we've never tested before in China, and then return them for sale in America. It's too expensive. I wouldn't even know how to quote you a price. Forget about it."

Such fears of operational complexity were also understandable. I didn't know anyone at the time who imported materials to China, blended them with indigenously sourced products (petroleum wax in my case), and shipped them back to America. Because of my new candles' design intricacy, I could only place orders for one 20-foot container of inventory at a time. This Chinese manufacturing facility was typical of many in favoring large, stable orders—it was accustomed to multiple 40-foot containers' worth of inventory per order. They roundly dismissed my new product.

Following this dispiriting meeting, I drove in silence to Hangzhou and complained to my sister, Li. By that time, my sister and her husband had welcomed a daughter into their family, occupied a modest two-bedroom apartment, and had become business partners with me and David. One year prior, while discussing the glow-candle business with them, I came to realize that I wasn't the only one in the family who dreamed of entrepreneurial stardom. They wanted in on the action. My brother-in-law had served as a professor of mathematics in Hangzhou University, while Li had worked for a factory that manufactured computers in the city. They earned a basic living but aspired to more.

Hangzhou had likely inspired their interest as well, for at the time our hometown was fast becoming an entrepreneurial mecca. While the Chinese economy began to open in the late 1970s, it didn't accelerate until the early 1990s, following Party Secretary Deng Xiaoping's promotion of his economic liberalization agenda during his famous 1992 southern tour through China. Just three years later, China exported textiles and all varieties of electronics, ranging from decorative Christmas lights to high-tech computers. In the mid-1990s, I also saw trendier and more niche fashion, fabric, and home décor startups sprouting up across Hangzhou. By 1999, these companies would find a much larger marketplace when Jack Ma and a group of friends convened in his Hangzhou apartment and founded Alibaba, now the world's largest ecommerce and retail company.

Finding such marketplace success represented a profound change in China. Historically, education was the only way to achieve social mobility. And education really meant performing well on examinations. During the millennia of Chinese imperial rule, the only way to receive a court or military position was through noble birth or successful test-taking, a tradition that devalued commerce and merchants. The advent of communism in China didn't change this general prejudice. Even after 1953, when Chairman Mao announced his First Five-Year Plan, aimed at modernizing and industrializing China's agrarian economy, factory workers took pride of place, once again at merchants' expense. Unlike farmers, soldiers, or factory workers, merchants weren't perceived as generating value for society. Instead, as the thinking went, they merely acted as third-party traders, buying products and reselling them at elevated prices.

In fairness, David and I affirmed these longstanding anti-merchant prejudices in our first foray into business. We traveled to China to find materials to trade in the American market and then hatched our glow-candle business. This was destined to be a short-lived operation because you can't succeed over the long term by following a trend or merely trading products at a markup. To be successful, I would later learn, I needed to add value at every single place in the supply chain, continuing to hone and resharpen my skills and capacities in the process.

My sister and her husband had initially dreamed of capitalizing on China's electronics boom by leveraging their computer-technology background to open a consulting business. Instead they started a modest factory to manufacture our magic glow candles in 1995. As Li heard me complain two years later about my lack of collaborators and willing partners for my new fragrance-infused candles, she looked at me, intrigued, and said, "What would it take to make the new fragrance candle in my factory? What do you need?"

I showed her my samples and conveyed the obstacles I faced. I needed manufacturers willing to work with my imported fragrances and then to ship small batch orders to the United States. Unlike the glow-candle operation, this would entail much larger capital investment, more factory-floor space, and significant financial risk.

Neither my sister nor I had advanced manufacturing experience, industrial machinery expertise, or background in establishing design-based protocols to run such a factory. But I give my sister a lot of credit. She called her husband that afternoon, explained the idea of fragrant candle-making to him, and soon thereafter, they updated their manufacturing facility for Chesapeake Bay candles in Hangzhou. Working with family is tricky, and my professional relationship with Li was wonderful and fulfilling on some days and tense and strained on others. To avoid misunderstandings and to preserve the entrepreneurial nature of the enterprise for all parties, I never structured our relationship as a merger. Instead, we formed a partnership. My sister and her husband incorporated and ran their own company, creating and manufacturing our candle products and then selling the finished products to Chesapeake Bay for distribution and sale.

Enlisting my sister and brother-in-law as collaborators was pivotal, but we still lacked capital. Chinese venture capitalists in the mid-1990s seeded and funded promising schemes and big ideas, but they largely favored major innovations in high tech or in the biomedical sciences. Anti-merchant prejudice persisted in the venture space, and

I had partially internalized it, too. Sometimes I was ashamed to say that my new business sold candles. When I did pitch my idea to investors, I received puzzled looks.

"You do what? You sell what?"

"I sell fragrant candles," I often replied.

"Yes, but what do they do?"

I figured that if investors asked about my candles' function, I was talking to the wrong people. I stopped seeking investment, and instead my family members borrowed money at 10 to 15 percent interest rates.

We bootstrapped this fragrant-candle operation, managing to accumulate $1 million in high-interest lending and personal savings to equip our small factory, located on the outskirts of Hangzhou, to manufacture our new products that summer. My father, who had worked in a factory setting his entire life, had made the biggest nonfinancial contribution to the operation when several years earlier he'd found us an abandoned manufacturing facility located about 30 minutes north of my parents' Hangzhou apartment, near the iron and steel mill where he'd once worked. Farmers in the area, who longed to generate additional money, had established these small warehouses on their lands over the course of China's industrial expansion, transforming the region into a manufacturing zone. Securing this facility was a major milestone, but I hardly remember the factory itself because it was unremarkable, located on a modest compound of land and consisting of a simple, open-plan, single-floor warehouse with a few enclosed office spaces radiating out.

Establishing production in this modest facility was even more daunting than raising this high-interest capital because I needed to somehow convert my basement operation to an industrial-scale candle-making enterprise. My dad tapped his network and we hired an experienced general manager, along with about 20 entry-level workers.

To ensure the quality of our product, my utmost concern, we began our industrial operations by creating a burn lab on the factory floor. For as many as six days a week, we burned every single color/dye formula in our portfolio around the clock. This helped us gauge the durability and consistency of our candle wicks and establish even and stable burn times. Such product consistency was difficult to achieve with petroleum wax, also known as paraffin wax. You might be tempted to think of petroleum wax, the byproduct of oil refinement, as a dirty substance. It's actually clean and an ideal medium for expressing color and transmitting fragrance. It's dominated candle-making ever since the early nineteenth century, when German chemist Carl Reichenback pioneered wax candles, replacing the acrid-smelling and poorly performing tallow (or animal fat) candles that had been fashionable in the west for centuries.[1]

Engineers monitoring the burn lab at the Chinese factory (2004).

But petroleum wax poses obstacles for candlemakers. We sourced our wax from northeast China, where agricultural minerals and natural-gas deposits supplied the country with its energy and caloric needs, and where my mom was once dispatched to labor camp. The wax from this region's diverse oil fields and refineries arrived to us in uneven white chunks that resembled large, lightweight rocks. Though they were always accompanied by the label "highly refined," we could sometimes smell notes of gas in our wax. Imagine trying to infuse subtle botanical fragrances into wax that smelled like gasoline!

Sometimes the quality varied regionally; some batches from the country's northeast, for example, might arrive caked in dirt, while those from the northwest might possess greater purity. On many occasions we received products of varying quality from the same refinery. Such inconsistencies in our core product ingredient altered our melting points, and by extension, our candles' performance. Even following many technological breakthroughs since the late twentieth century, it's still difficult to standardize wax.

But even after achieving some consistency, the interaction of wax with fragrance oils and dyes always influences a candle's burn behavior. Our fragrance stabilities varied, too, also influencing burn times. Take every candlemaker's workhorse product: the white vanilla candle. Vanilla is a global staple, omnipresent in foods like French vanilla ice cream and consumer offerings like vanilla bean moisturizing lotion. But vanilla is a rare crop, mainly grown in Madagascar and Réunion. Vanilla beans' strength and potency vary as rainfall, sun exposure, and other such variables alter each seasonal harvest. Just like weather affects the growth of grapes and adds endless complexity to wines, so do naturally sourced products like vanilla, affecting fragrance notes, candle burn times, and general performance. Given the variable biochemistry of each wax batch, coupled with the complexity of different oil and color combinations, our product-control managers had to constantly modify our formulas.

Following their preproduction observations and experiments in the burn lab, our workers generated candle samples for our Maryland office that we in turn brandished during retail meetings and trade shows. Only two weeks into our factory operations for fragrant candles, in the winter of 1996, our preproduction crew instituted an invaluable policy: we needed to perform non-draft burn tests. That meant that the burn lab needed to be far from any air conditioning vents, as drafts made it impossible for candles to burn evenly. We converted our burn laboratory into a small fragrance box, situating it within a 4x2-foot glass enclosure, entirely sealed except for a small aperture covered with a hanging mat. There, we could insert our heads, observe the candles, and breath in the fragrances.

That winter our production process slowly took shape. We melted oversize wax stones and promptly transferred them to smaller vats that glided along the factory floor on wheeled trolleys. Factory workers received these rolling carrousels, applying color and fragrance to the trolley cart from a glass dial before pushing them down the assembly line. Other workers received the incoming trolleys, now saturated with a signature Chesapeake Bay color and olfactory mixture, transferring their hot wax concoctions to individually handcrafted metal candle molds. The candles then cooled for 8–10 hours. After the wax solidified, workers drilled a hole into each candle bottom, enabling them to snake a wick through the wax. They then polished the completed candle, coated them with shrink wrap, applied our label, and packaged them for shipment.

My sister and I, along with our entire crew, learned our most valuable manufacturing lessons from the greatest teacher of all: failure. One day in the winter of 1996, we accidentally set our wax melting temperatures so high that entire wax batches lacked any hint of our trademark fragrances. We'd burned the scents right off! On other occasions, our distinctive fragrance and dye formulas led to oil oozing from the wax ("bleeding"), the blackening of the candle wax along the products' edges, and, once again, to inconsistent burn times. Through trial and error, we learned about production and cooling lines, how to properly heat and store the fragrances and wax, how to straighten our candle wicks, and how to create stable products that retained their uniqueness while achieving consistent lifecycles. We gradually created standard operating procedures, learning from mistakes we made with shipping, inventory- and supply-chain management, and purchasing. Not to suggest that our early operation was state of the art—our wax warehouse was really the outdoor ground behind our office building. We stacked the wax there in shipping bags, shielding it from the elements with a tarp.

As we labored away, constantly updating our standard operating procedures based on mistakes we'd committed, we understood how improbable this venture was. Most businesspeople failed, even those with substantially more money and expertise than ours. But I intuitively knew that if we somehow managed to succeed, manufacturing would be one of our core market differentiators. After all, most small and mid-size American candle brands, just like most lotion and potion brands, outsourced manufacturing to original equipment manufacturing (OEM) companies.

Most critically for me, parting with manufacturing meant parting with innovation. If you don't control manufacturing, labeling and packaging are the only ways to distinguish yourself in the market. And while the latter were crucial for me, innovating with fragrance, texture, and color was key to my product identity. I couldn't do that without controlling, and eventually mastering, the manufacturing process.

What Chesapeake Bay lacked in manufacturing experience and investment capital, we made up for in marketing. With the glow-candle company, I'd accumulated about 600 customers. This constellation of mom-and-pop stores spanned the entire country and provided me with a large swath of potential vendors. Every shop on my mailing list received a glossy brochure embossed with images of the new candles, complete with my new logo. I hoped to launch the candles by converting a fraction of these glow-candle vendors into Chesapeake Bay vendors. From our warehouse in the industrial zone of Upper Marlboro, Maryland, we waited for vendors to place orders. Gradually, these phone and fax orders trickled in.

Mei and her design team poised for a new product launch (2007).

My sister, Li, shipped Chesapeake Bay's first candle batch early in 1997. In Maryland, we eagerly gathered around this 20-foot container, unpacked the pallets within it, and filled our first orders for mom-and-pop stores across the country.

We achieved an early and most gratifying victory in the first months of Chinese production, landing a deal with Bloomingdale's. I'd approached the buyers of this iconic department store in the summer of 1996, and they'd agreed to an order. But it wasn't until spring of 1997, when I ventured back to Bloomingdale's in New York City to see my own products, that I felt the impact of this deal. In anticipation of spring, the store merchandizers gravitated to my lime green and white candles, and I spotted them as soon as I took the escalator to the home floor. As I navigated deeper into the aisles, I continued seeing my candles. To my amazement, merchandizers at Bloomingdale's didn't confine my product to a single shelf or confined area, like they did for Gucci designer handbags or Dolce & Gabbana cocktail dresses. Instead, they'd lined them inside kitchen cabinets and alongside dinnerware, positioned them atop living room tables and nearby fine English Wedgwood porcelain tea sets, and tastefully arrayed them on bedroom end tables and bathroom shelves. I saw candle clusters at different heights and angles, their staggered appearance serving as a miniature work of art that made the store's furniture radiate with the energy of spring and its promise of renewal.

Witnessing such cross-merchandising of my product, which made such a bold lifestyle statement, should have left me exhilarated. This was the place I'd hatched my scheme of transforming the home décor space with an aesthetic that I'd spotted in women's fashion. And now I witnessed my vision brought to life; my fresh and bold green and white candles, resembling green apples and white tulips, were making this already chic department store pop. Not only had my dream been realized, but my favorite store—the one that had served as my refuge and safe harbor during my bleak time in New York—had not only purchased my products but had made them omnipresent throughout its store's home department. Bloomingdale's had stature and exercised cultural influence, and its display shelves served as educational guides for trendy New Yorkers on how to tastefully decorate their homes. I realized that day that my products were destined to appear in New York apartments that season, uneven clusters adding zest to a bathroom, and linear ones suggesting order and balance to families sitting down at the table to eat dinner.

Among my family members, nobody was better positioned to enjoy the moment than me. My sister had never ventured outside of China and couldn't appreciate a store like Bloomingdale's. Neither could my factory-oriented father. I took a moment to bask in the pride. But only a moment. Even as I'd achieved an extraordinary personal and professional milestone that day, I knew how easily seasonal cycles and trends ebbed and flowed. Bloomindale's buyers, just like the public, were fickle, their changing tastes rendering once-popular brands suddenly passé and irrelevant. So instead of allowing myself to stop and enjoy, my mind was already moving far into the future, thinking of ways I could keep my product trendy and compelling for seasons to come.

Chesapeake Rising

Bloomingdale's paved the way for more major retailer deals like Nordstrom and Bed Bath & Beyond, two national retailers that I cinched in 1997. I was pleased to have them both. Nordstrom was another blue-chip department store famous for its high-end cosmetics and women's shoe offerings. Its home department was underdeveloped, which meant that landing the deal wasn't a huge impact to our business in terms of volume, though having it on our client list was priceless. Bed Bath & Beyond had always fascinated me. I routinely shook my head, having entered the store just to browse the current offerings and then leaving with cutting boards, cleaning devices with enticing new designs, and little plastic gadgets that made thin zucchini noodles that resembled actual pasta. Unlike Nordstrom, this company keenly understood the home space, mobilizing new innovation and emerging ideas (like zoodles) that drove incremental sales in their stores.

Prior to the advent of Amazon, the American consumer industry was more chaotic, making it hard for small vendors like me to work with the big box stores that dominated the retail space. Take Bed Bath & Beyond, where, I learned after signing our deal, individual managers at each box store location made purchasing and reordering decisions on their own, without considering regional trends or larger chain inventories. Once these stores printed their orders, all of which had staggered quantities, we then spread them out in large fields outside of our warehouse, where every individual store was indicated with a sign and its individual quantities grouped nearby. Doing that for 200 to 300 stores was labor-intensive, extremely cumbersome, and rife with error. If we miscounted, store managers and salespeople called us to complain, demanding replacements or discounts for the inconvenience—something that cut into our already slim margins. Sometimes the nonuniformity and uniqueness of our products posed problems. We infused a lot of fragrances into our early product lines, and sometimes these candles bled on the shelf, oozing yellow, green, or pink tear-shaped secretions as they sweltered in the hot summer sun. This frustrated store managers and consumers alike.

Even when everything went according to plan and the stores received their exact orders of quality products, they needed to promptly take stock of inventory or we'd never receive a reorder. Not that we exerted any influence in the arrangement or merchandizing of our products;

that was the exclusive purview of store managers. And while Bed Bath & Beyond was great at embracing novelty, they often crowded their displays, leaving some products lost in the shuffle. Natural products often suffered this fate, losing limelight to louder, shiner objects on the display shelf.

In the predigital era, moreover, many stores knew little about their sales numbers and customer bases. Though every major retailer had databases that tracked inventory according to vendor sales data, such information wasn't typically current or segmented by store. That meant that I might have sold 200 vanilla candles throughout the Nordstrom chain one year, but I had no inkling about which stores or regions in which they were popular. Maybe stores in Florida and California gravitated to a specific color or scent, but I'd never know. This lack of precision wasn't retailers' fault; this was simply prior to the era of big data, customer segmentation, and advanced analytics. Most stores worked from sales report spreadsheets that they printed every Monday and used their background and intuition to guide purchasing decisions.

As a seasonal vendor for most of my big retailers, I waited for the two major buying seasons of spring and fall to gauge my product's popularity. We usually worked with our buyers on an advance 12-month cycle, ordering 1 year out to budget sufficient time for manufacturing, planning, and delivery that year. Spring is a major retail season—the post-holiday retail slump comes to an end and people begin buying for spring and summer. The fall season is even bigger, as people begin buying for back to school, a new home décor season, cold weather gear, fashionable items for holiday parties, and the Christmas season. About 60 percent of my business occurred during this September-to-December "Falliday" season.

In an ideal year, I'd sell down my spring inventory by late summer, making my retail customers eager to replenish their stocks for Falliday. But if my seasonal sell-through—a consumer retailer term referring to the percentage of inventory that is sold after being shipped from a supplier—was low, box stores reduced their reorders. And that imperiled my product's survival at the company as consumers forgot about the fragranced candles they'd ordered last season.

Promotions further complicated sell-throughs. If a store offered a discount promotion timed for a certain holiday, they expected increased sales to compensate for the price reduction. If we couldn't sell out our inventory when prices were reduced, we were in real trouble. Sometimes my seasonal sell-through was high, and my customers reordered. But sometimes my customers purchased for spring, and when August rolled around, they still had half of my inventory in stock. Not only were my sales disappointing, but the retailers now had to store my unsold merchandise, precisely when they wanted to make room in the warehouses and store shelves for Falliday.

Most companies were small seasonal vendors like me who dreamed of becoming replenishing vendors for large retailers. Seasonal merchandising was difficult on retailers and vendors alike. If a large box store made one seasonal order for Christmas tree lights, for example, it couldn't make reorders based on consumer demand. Lacking continued data about product demand, these manufacturers never learned about their products' consumer appeal. Replenishment vendors like P&G, General Mills, or Johnson & Johnson, by contrast, had offerings like Tide, Cheerios, and baby lotion that required continual replenishment schedules. I technically obtained the replenishment vendor status with Bed Bath & Beyond in 1997, but absent data analytics our inventory and reorders were always hit-or-miss, and I still felt like a seasonal vendor.

I never had a true gauge of how we were actually performing.

Right on Target

During my spare time outside of the office, I constantly traveled to retail stores, scoping out the competition and spotting new design trends. And like many people in the late 1990s, I became increasingly attracted to Target. This Minneapolis-based retail chain, which began in the 1960s, had swelled to around 800 locations throughout the country. Hailing from the Midwest, Target's founders had a largely northern European aesthetic that was spare and minimal while also stylish and fun. For that reason, the retail giant was beginning to acquire a trendy reputation among consumers, who pronounced the company's name with a faux French accent—*Tar-JHAY*—or even referred to it as Neiman Target.

When I traveled to my local Target in Maryland in late 1996, the contemporary design immediately appealed to me. I liked the racetrack layout, with one large aisle guiding customers around each store's perimeter, as well as Target's bull's-eye logo signs of white-infused crimson, leading shoppers to its various departments in the store's interior.[2] Their shelves were tastefully spaced, their lighting friendly and bright, and while aisles were dense with products, they retained an uncluttered feel. Target products were also playful and fun, like animal-print towels, tie-dyed polyester shower curtains, affordable men's track suits, and single-striped women's bikinis that looked just as stylish as designer suits from an upscale Parisian boutique.

Navigating my way from the adorable onesies and childhood gifts, I ventured to Target's candle offerings. Even in late 1996, the store devoted an entire "valley" to candles, which refers to two 20-foot facing aisles, flanked by four endcaps (the smaller shelves that face major pedestrian walkways around the store's interior). Endcaps are expensive retail real estate and are usually more trend-driven, designed to appeal to shoppers who might take interest in the latest designs but have no desire to stroll the candle valley.

As I looked at this staggering volume of products, I was struck by how much candle-making had matured over the decade. The candle industry saw double-digit growth every year in the 1990s, and now featured different designs, materials, holders, and accompanying accessories like tealights—circular deposits of wax, housed within metal or clear PVC containers—and fragranced crystal beads. Walking the aisles, I was struck by how fragranced candles in different sizes with intricate designs had replaced the long, scentless tapers that had once exclusively graced American dinner tables and nightstands. I could even see interested shoppers take notice of circular and rounded "pillar" candles tastefully arrayed on the candle valley's endcaps.

Around the time I began these explorations, Target made the fateful decision to partner with famous American architect Michael Graves. After marveling at Michael Graves's unique architectural solutions and industrial designs, Ron Johnson, a Target vice president overseeing home décor, made Graves its first in-house designer.[3] This monumental partnership would cement Target's reputation as a stylish alternative to Kmart and Walmart, and make Michael Graves a household name.

In the late 1990s, when Michael Graves helped position Target at the forefront of the democratic design movement, I couldn't help but think that this was exactly where I belonged, too. Like Graves, I wasn't trained as a designer but instead gravitated to contemporary aesthetics. I naturally embraced a "democratization of design" philosophy, enabling broad consumer access to stylish products. Target also represented an incredible business opportunity for any vendor. At over 800 stores, it was larger than my other major retailers like Bed Bath & Beyond. Better yet, Target dedicated considerable real estate to design-driven home goods. I marveled at the exclusive Michael Graves kitchenware items, like tea kettles and serving spoons, that cost a fraction of the high-design price but were collectibles and designed for Target with an architect's eye to form and function. My mind began imagining the collections I could make for Target and how my bright-colored contemporary trends would dovetail with the animal-print bathrobes that people purchased. I realized I'd gone into business for the same reason as Target: to deliver stylish, contemporary, and chic design-driven goods at everyday, affordable price points.

In late 1996, I brushed off the Yellow Pages in my living room and found the phone number for the Target Corporation. I navigated my way through the phone tree to the candle buyer and left her a message. She didn't return my call. I didn't want to come off as a stalker, so for the next five weeks, I left her one message every week: "Hello, my name is Mei, I'm based in Maryland, and I have a very modern, contemporary candle line that would be great for your store."

After this didn't work, I decided to call her secretary, and see if I had the wrong number or the wrong person. In retrospect, this was very naïve. "It's every buyer's job to answer calls," explained the secretary. "When they don't, sometimes we just give you the supervisor. Let me connect you."

After contacting the supervisor, the candle buyer returned my call, clearly insulted that I'd gone over her head. "If you want to establish a relationship, you are off to a bad start," she scolded.

Her boss had clearly given her an earful for her lack of professionalism, and I should have anticipated that reaction. I didn't envy that buyer's job. She probably received tens of thousands of calls and emails every week from hopeful vendors like me who dreamed of having their products grace the store's ample shelves. And I was reaching out during the high-sales and high-stress Falliday season. I hung up the phone a little dejected, thinking that I'd permanently alienated the Target buyer and doomed any chance of partnership.

But one Tuesday afternoon, in March 1997, I decided to call the same number again, only to discover that the buyer had changed. As the message box indicated, the new buyer was a young and friendly person named Jennifer Schock. Her prerecorded message gave me positive vibes, as she sounded fresh out of college, excited to have landed her first job, and ambitious to make a name for herself. I left a cheerful message in return, reflecting this same spirit.

I nearly fell off my chair two days later when she called, telling me how impressed she was by the description of the product and how she wanted to arrange a meeting to see some samples. This wasn't a typical response, as most buyers—if they returned your call at all—gave you a lackluster sigh, instructed you to "send some samples," or maybe asked for a brochure and price point. You usually never hear from them after that. If you managed to secure an appointment, it was typically scheduled for three months out, an eternity for the fast-paced retail calendar responding to constantly changing consumer tastes. Without ever having seen a sample, Jennifer wanted to see me and my products in two weeks!

Given Target's reputation for fashion, I decided to spruce up my color palette with some unique colors and designs, just as I had when pitching Bloomingdale's, Nordstrom, and Bed Bath & Beyond. I designed 10 colors that would come in 6 different sizes each, with squat and short offerings alongside long and lanky ones, and with some fragrance staples (like vanilla) and some innovative offerings (like orange mint). To make a splash, I designed a 6x6-inch candle with 3 wicks that boasted a total burn time of 600 hours. American homes are big, I figured, and one flame just wasn't always enough. To accomplish this visual and fragrance-based statement, I drew on my creative side and flair for the dramatic—a burgeoning part of the personality that would only grow as I gained confidence in my ability to use color, fragrance, texture, and form in product design.

I was nervous and a little giddy preparing for my meeting with Jennifer Schock later that April. I reached out to a few cosmetic vendors who partnered with Target and they gave me some helpful, if sobering advice: "Your company is too small for them to roll you out in all of their stores. If you're lucky, they'll probably test you in 200."

I followed up by asking how big this 200-store test would be. "We do around $4 million a year with them in over 800 stores and we have over 100 SKUs," the person replied, referring to the alphanumeric codes that help identify each piece of unique inventory.

I kept these intimidating financials in mind that fateful April day in 1997 when I ventured, alone, to meet Jennifer. I deplaned a day early with two brown shipping boxes filled with samples. I couldn't entrust this precious cargo to any shipping company, because if the packages went missing, my meeting would be a flop. The following morning, I awoke fresh and began assembling a "chic and professional" outfit that I donned when meeting buyers. The style typically consisted of impeccably tailored Italian fabrics in neutral and solid colors, without any distracting patterns or prints. I also steered clear of brands and mint fashion labels and tried to leave people guessing where I purchased my clothing. To this day, once a celebrity hypes a fashion brand, I drop it in favor of something undiscovered.

Whenever I met a new buyer, local government official, or business associate, I gave considerable thought to my outfit, trying to select clothing that honored the person I was meeting and also gave me confidence. Knowing Jennifer was in her twenties and lived in Minneapolis, I decided to wear an orange jacket over a lightweight and sleeveless dove-gray wool dress. Over the years, this dress-plus-jacket combo had become a buyer-meeting staple, able to shine during the day and power me through the evening. That day, I paired it with a two-inch heel, conveying a midwestern chic—trying to show minimal effort without coming across as underdressed. I mustered my resolve, shepherded my two brown boxes down the Marriott hotel corridor, and ventured to Target's headquarters in the heart of downtown Minneapolis.

Jennifer greeted me with vivid eyes and a warmth that put me immediately at ease. Around 28 years old, she had a short bob of hair, flawless skin, and a radiant smile. She extended her hand and introduced herself, something I also appreciated because so many buyers were too busy to engage in pleasantries and instead rushed to see your product. Jennifer described how after serving as a merchandiser for several years, she had just become a Target buyer. As I'd later learn, this was a typical trajectory. Target routinely hired recent graduates from Midwestern universities in Indiana, Ohio, and Wisconsin and assigned them the role of analysts, responsible for reporting weekly sales and placing orders. Those who excelled in that role and mastered a product cycle then received promotions to assistant buyers. To ascend the ranks to bona fide buyer they needed to prove their mettle in a product category, which often represented 200–300 million in annual buying dollars. For a recent college graduate in her twenties, this was a tremendous responsibility and honor.

As I gave Jennifer a rundown of Chesapeake Bay, I emphasized the unique designs that came from our Chinese manufacturing facility. Most buyers that I'd worked with remained stonefaced and slumped in their seats during meetings, either because they wanted to shield their interest or because they were genuinely skeptical of the product. Jennifer was the opposite, and I saw her excitement grow with my explanations, which infused me with confidence. She couldn't wait to get up and test the product. I capitalized on Jennifer's eagerness and energy, pointing the bottom of the candles toward her nose so she could sniff the fragrance. This is how a professional candle buyer becomes acquainted with fragrant candles, much like sommeliers who whirl a glass of wine to discern its legs and then plunge their noses into their glasses, seeking to detect the various fragrance notes. She inquired about the pricing, complimented the 10 colors I'd featured that day, and unconsciously started to arrange the products on mock shelves, as if merchandizing on the store floor.

"How soon can you deliver them?" she asked, taking her gaze away from the products and looking me straight in the eye.

I tried not to gasp. I'd met with buyers from Bloomingdale's and Bed Bath & Beyond, and most waited days or weeks to give me an affirmative answer. Jennifer had asked for a delivery in the first 20 minutes of our meeting!

"You mean in 200 stores?" I pressed, thinking I was being provocative and trying to subtly reveal how well-educated I was about Target's new vendor-testing practices.

"No, all 800," she countered, a faint smile forming on her lips.

Now I really had to stabilize myself, gripping the arms of my chair for leverage as the room began to spin. I calculated the numbers: this would be a $1 million seasonal order. My mind immediately began racing. Could my modest operation, consisting of a small Chinese factory and Maryland-based team of around 10 people, possibly sign with one of the biggest retailers in the world? Sure, we had 2,000 mom-and-pop retailers, and 3 chain stores, but we'd never sold to a company with a footprint as big as Target.

It was now April. Even if the Chinese factory immediately ramped up production, did I really have the people, shipping capacity, and even molds, dyes, and fragrances on hand to deliver on this scale?

"Probably October," I blurted out.

"Perfect," she replied without missing a beat. "If you're shipping from China, that means the order should arrive here in December, and your products will be on shelves just in time for the New Year."

"By the way," she said as I turned to leave, "I'm giving you four feet at the lead cap."

I was stunned. The lead cap is the initial section of a store aisle, where shoppers can glimpse your merchandise from the large perimeter halls. It's second only to the highly coveted, expensive endcap real estate.

Somehow, I managed to hail a taxi, and as I saw the Marriott hotel flash by en route to the airport, I gave the hotel a bow and prayer of thanks. In Buddhist tradition, this is a sign of appreciation and respect for people and places that nurture and support you along life's journey. For every following trip to Target, I promised myself, I would stay at a Marriott.

Jennifer called with more good news the following week, indicating that her boss saw the samples, the whole team loved them, and they all eagerly awaited the first arrival. And here's where the Target relationship proved decisive. Because of the company's focus on design and quality differentiation from its big competitors like Kmart and Walmart, it contracted with many small and innovative vendors. And Target knew that, because these vendors were small and specialized, most lacked the logistical capability and organizational acumen to deliver at the scale and magnitude that the retail behemoth required.

Instead of hiding these operational challenges, Target proactively broached them, enrolling each of its new vendors into a comprehensive onboarding program. As I prepared my first order, I began this training, which transformed me into a true partner and Target collaborator. Together with a handful of other new vendors in the home décor space, I learned about the store's gigantic headquarters in Minneapolis, Minnesota, where the weather is so cold that most of the downtown is located within 10 blocks of the city center and connected via enclosed skyways. It was here, I learned, that employees converged to create a roadmap or "planogram" of each store.

Visual merchandisers worked alongside creatives to maximize the allure of each regional and demographic market. Florida stores, for example, have an older demographic base in need of gear for warmer weather, while more rural and suburban stores in the American interior have younger customer bases and might need more baby clothing and children's toys. Some wealthy, high-traffic stores in Southern California received more inventory and had more shelves to fill, while some in more rural parts of the country weren't as popular and received reduced loads to accommodate more modest sales forecasts. The planogram gave Target a distinct company look that made it predictable, but not corporate in feel.

Understanding these diverse geographies, projected sales, and the peaks and valleys of customer behavior was enormously helpful. For the first time when working with major retailers, I could plan my raw material orders for fragrances, labels, and wax. I was also now equipped to handle the most important operational component of all: people. Without understanding customer behavior projections, supply-chain disruptions ran rampant, as we laid off workers when demand decreased but then furiously rehired them when it picked up. Understanding the calendar-based dynamism of customer appeal allowed our company to dedicate the April-to-June period to training new workers, and the later summer to broadening their abilities to perform more complex responsibilities, readying them for increased manufacturing demand later that year. Perhaps manufacturing would have stayed in the United States, I remember thinking during my onboarding, if everyone had a partner like Target, providing reliable business forecasts and support.

During these vendor trainings, I witnessed how Target's cutting-edge supply-chain management systems could nimbly respond to consumer demand. At the distribution centers, we witnessed large electronic arms sort our products into individual trucks. Unlike other major retailers, Target has never equipped its stores with warehouse space. Every Target truck you see on the freeway each day is likely coming from a distribution center and going to replenish a single store with any missing daily inventory, and each of those trucks is physically unloaded at every store. That means that if the order is wrong or if the inventory is damaged, there is no recourse to an on-site warehouse.

This lean product-supply model burdened Target's inventory management technologies and its vendors alike. Watching product pallets being loaded into trucks, and imagining them being offloaded in individual stores, I could imagine how one big error could really disrupt operations. The wrong order could result in a planogram hole, leading to financial losses and reduced customer confidence. If we put financial strain like that on our stores, we learned, we would receive a "chargeback," meaning we'd have to pay for the mistake. If we'd incorrectly weighed our materials when the truck picked them up, we'd receive a freight chargeback of anywhere from several hundred to several thousand dollars. The bigger the retail loss, the bigger the chargeback. The same happened if our barcodes were unscannable, or if we weren't ready to ship when the distribution truck arrived. But our onboarding managers didn't tell us this to scare us. The entire training process was designed to help us to proactively identify problems and prevent errors.

First team of Target buyers visit the China factory (1997); from left to right: David Wang, Mei, Li, Jennifer Schock, Tom (Li's husband), and a senior Target buyer.

As a new Target vendor, ramping up overseas production ahead of my first order, I felt a healthy sense of humility. On the one hand, I had confidence in my colors, fragrances, and labels. I also provided an affordable luxury that perfectly aligned with Target's larger value proposition. But this operational complexity and sheer scale was of a different magnitude than anything I'd experienced. I'd worked with large department stores at much lower volumes, and these operations lacked the technology, attention to detail, and innovative business model to approach purchasing and distribution with such precision. I often didn't have clarity on my sales at Nordstrom or Bloomingdale's and neither did these department stores, which sometimes purchased entire seasonal collections from designers like Michael Kors, resulting in huge end-of-season markdowns for unpopular pieces, and loss of margins for both retailer and vendor. Target, by contrast, placed more conservative initial orders and gauged reorders based on weekly storewide sell-through reports. Because it catered to a large, less elitist market, the store could transform our candles into everyday American items. But if I disappointed Target with an error, I would share the destiny of many other promising vendors, who despite the help and resources Target provided, couldn't rise to the rank of partner.

A Date with Destiny

In late October, our first Target-bound shipping containers departed from Shanghai's port and began their voyage to Baltimore. Because we were so inexperienced, we couldn't imagine the size and scope of the first order, let alone prepare for it. Imagine: we produced and filled 20 massive shipping containers to capacity. Have you ever seen the huge 40-foot trucks on the freeway bearing the contents of one such container? They're intimidating, leaving you unable to see surrounding traffic if you drive behind them.

The finished products for that first Target order had accumulated in China until the factory was crowded with inventory and line workers competed for elbow space on the floor. Unfortunately, it was costly to ship small batches as they came off the factory floor, and we didn't have a U.S.-based warehouse large enough to store them anyway. Luckily for us, but sadly for the state of American manufacturing, we found many abandoned warehouses and shuttered factories in the DC area that fall. This left us some vacancies for an affordable, short-term rental. We found a warehouse 10 times larger than ours nearby and rented it for two weeks. The landlord seemed perplexed about this temporary rental, but he didn't pry.

That was for the best as I couldn't have possibly explained to him that we needed his warehouse to receive our set order from China, meticulously unpack it, reassemble it according to our purchase orders, and ready it for delivery to 20 different distribution centers from where it would enter 800 individual Target stores. I buckled as I thought about my onboarding trip to the distribution center, seeing the automatic product scanners reject perfectly fine products with unclear labels. Target received such a vast array of inventory that if machines and workers couldn't distinguish candles from cosmetics, the offending vendors might be replaced. And even if products were successfully scanned and redistributed, each store had to receive its unique combination of eight colors, sizes, and fragrances to occupy four feet and five shelves of real estate at the beginning of every candle valley.

As I learned from my first Target order, even if you have a cadre of well-trained and highly motivated employees on the factory and office floors, all anticipating your order and primed for success, you'll inevitably encounter glitches. Our first glitch that October was shipment delays. Our small company usually shipped two containers from China but now had 20 containers on U.S. soil, something that piqued the interest of American customs' officials. They organized an impromptu inspection, scrutinizing our shipping information, verifying that we'd paid our tariffs, and ensuring we hadn't included any contraband alongside our merchandise. In addition to delaying our productivity and time to market, we now had to pay for bureaucrats to perform their inspections.

We bit our nails, hoping the government would expedite its inspection, each hour that elapsed eating into our already tight turnaround time for reshipment. When the 20 containers finally pulled up to our facility, our slim week window for redistribution was reduced to 3 days. If we didn't repackage everything and ship in that narrow timeframe, we'd be penalized. And remember the nearby warehouse we'd rented to store and process this initial order? It was so temporary that we didn't think to equip it with electricity. We'd figured we'd take a week to unload all of these pallets and rearrange them during the workday.

My anxiety was through the roof. There was a reason that I occupied the front end and not the back end of the business. Sure, I was good at design and skilled at negotiating with buyers. But if I had to deal with inventories, shipment delays, and manufacturing hiccups, I'd worry myself to death. But no one on the back-end team, including my sister, David, or Richard, had communicated the urgency or even despair that they felt at fulfilling this Target order until days before the trucks finally pulled up that late fall night. Whenever I'd inquired about the order, they'd reassured me, saying, "We're fine. It's left China and will be arriving soon."

Blissful in my ignorance, I'd been relaying these confident messages to Jennifer, all the while broaching the topics of holiday season orders and new Falliday designs.

I froze. Our fate hinged on this first shipment. I was momentarily paralyzed as I thought of the hundreds of people who were counting on us. This included our dedicated workers on the factory floor in China; each merchandizer at Target, looking to arrange that four feet of real estate in a way to attract customers; and Jennifer Schock, the young buyer who'd taken a chance on me and whose reputation was also on the line. The overwhelming volume of merchandise before me only exacerbated my anxiety. As each container made its way into the warehouse, I came to grips with the sheer volume of this order. Forget the gentle unloading and repackaging of the materials I had initially envisaged. Marathon runners in peak condition likely lacked the stamina to fulfill this order, even if they worked around the clock.

It was 5:00 p.m. on a cold, pitch-black November evening when we began unloading our merchandise and gradually realized that we lacked electricity. Activating our immigrant instincts, we devised a makeshift solution. David and Richard drove their cars into the warehouse, kept the engines running, and turned on their headlights and high beams, enabling us to see the product. We worked all night, one warehouse worker manning a forklift and the rest of us disassembling pallets and repacking them for reshipment. I remember how exhausted we were the next morning, especially when I spoke with our secretary and warehouse workers, desperately trying to work out logistics. Several of the drivers coming to retrieve this merchandise lost their way en route to our remote warehouse, and prior to cellular phone technology, we had to repeat instructions of how to arrive at our industrial park as they scribbled them on a piece of paper from a public payphone.

We worked around the clock for 72 hours, powered by adrenaline and illuminated by the headlights of our cars. We were as careful and meticulous as we were exhausted. We unloaded and relabeled hundreds of pallets; surely, we'd make a mistake at some point, I fretted. After that burst of activity, when every last product had exited the warehouse, our collective nervousness only increased. The tornado had departed, leaving a deafening silence that engulfed our entire operation. We had no idea whether the materials had been received, and we couldn't pester our buyers, who were already overwhelmed in the pre-Christmas run-up.

As always, David and I ventured to Florida that holiday season, but I remained obsessed with this order. I poked into the local Target stores and didn't see any of our products in the candle valleys. I tried my best to put everything out of my mind, but really couldn't enjoy our annual trip down south.

Six weeks after the shipments, sometime during the third week of January 1998, Jennifer Schock left me a voice message: "Please call me back. We are in trouble."

You can imagine my sense of dread: visions of mislabeling, planograms in disarray, and customer complaints about the candles washed over me. I could hear the anxiety in her tone. I promptly returned her call and heard the desperation in her voice. "Mei, we're running out of stock."

She told me to return to China and increase production immediately. Our candle sales had exceeded Target's projections by 200 percent! I screamed involuntarily, overwhelming an enthusiastic but still low-key and measured Jennifer.

Chesapeake Maturing

At this moment, I wanted to scream, "Okay, we'll do it!" But I couldn't. My sister's factory was overwhelmed with the current orders, and there was no way she could ramp up production threefold. This great news of my product's popularity fell during Chinese New Year, when production usually decreases throughout the entire Mainland as people visit their families and celebrate. I was determined to get more product onto the shelves, but that required additional manufacturing facilities, experienced workers, and substantially more raw materials, labels, cartons, and fragrances.

Seeing this unprecedented response in customer demand for candles, a Target representative proactively reached out to my company. They congratulated us for hitting a nerve with American consumers but told us that the onboarding training was no longer enough, given that we'd transformed from a small to a mid-size Target vendor overnight. Both our company and Target stood to increase in profitability, they said, but to satisfy this demand we needed to scale our operation. We needed new inventory management systems, complete with different trigger points for reorders and larger industrial facilities with more workers. They strongly encouraged us to hire a representative broker to assist with this transformation and suggested Portu Sunberg, a Minneapolis-based consumer brand agency.

Chesapeake's decision to partner with Sunberg proved strategic, enabling us to meet our operational challenges along the growth process, while continually building trust and insight into Target's approach to design, trends, merchandising, and consumer behavior. This partnership also helped us navigate Target's famous buyer turnover. Like the diplomatic corps, Target buyers change positions every two years, and Jennifer would soon take her candle-buying knowledge and expertise to the retailer's garden business. Portu Sunberg's team helped us manage our transition to a new buyer, whom we introduced to the fragrance and candle-making industries. They also shared timely updates about Target programs and initiatives, ensuring that we never missed an opportunity.

With their help and guidance, we replenished our candle stocks and responded to the threefold increase in customer demand by April 1998.

But even with such strong support in place, problems always surface. For instance, one of our spring shipments arrived with upside-down candle labels. Easy mistake: no one in our factories could read English. In hindsight, we should have left multiple samples at the factory, so everyone had a physical copy of the product to consult. But instead of supplying these physical reference points, we'd simply emailed photographs of mock labels to office members. Such hiccups happen in multicultural environments, and we hadn't anticipated this one. We worked with a label vendor and rushed replacement labels to the United States. That spring, I hired a crew to remove every single candle from every single carton of the shipment affected, and painstakingly reapply each label.

Later that year, our Christmas candles created an even greater challenge. As we've seen, my vybar-less wax texture creates a snowflake appearance, which customers loved, because it made the candles natural and unique. My cinnamon apple fragrance candles with snowflakes would be even more special during the holidays, I'd reasoned when designing them, because cold and snow are integral to the mood and spirit. Target agreed and made a substantial order. But somehow that color, fragrance, and texture combination exercised an unusual effect on the texture, making snowflakes clump on certain sides while leaving other parts of the candle nude.

I received a panicked call from David Sunberg at Target's Minneapolis headquarters, fretting about the uneven distribution of snowflakes on these Christmas candles. Target managers had expressed concern, saying that the candle didn't resemble what they'd seen during their prior planogram walkthrough, and that this didn't speak well of Target's quality control. I called my sister and made plans with her to airship candles to replace any defective products.

The pressure mounted and I lost sleep that holiday season. As I furiously compared air shipping quotes, I realized that no matter whom I selected, this would turn any revenue projections into losses, adding an extra $10 to each candle cost. Everyone in Target's buying office was worried about the snowflakes, so to salvage this key partnership, I was willing to assume a major financial loss and ship candle replacements. But that Christmas season, red "snowflaked" candles began disappearing from store shelves, just as forecast, and not a single customer returned a candle for that reason. Target buyers had apparently underestimated Americans' desire for handmade products. Mercifully, we were spared the burden of air shipping. But the question of the snowflakes lingers among merchandizers and buyers to this day, partially because that drive for homogenization and uniformity persists in large-scale operations, even ones as design-forward as Target.

For 1998 we forecast $3.2 million in sales to Target. We tripled that figure, selling close to $9 million. To put this in perspective, we did $8 million in combined non-Target sales that year. I felt relieved and vindicated. I now reached a broad customer market and formed a small part of a larger change in consumer lifestyles. Customers the country over had spontaneously responded to my product, which struck them as fresh and contemporary—the affordable luxury they desired to enliven their spaces.

But success bred competition. Other candle makers walked the aisles of Target, just as I routinely had in prior years, looking for opportunities to offer cheaper versions of our products at lower margins. In every industry, some players never invent or innovate but instead seek market advantage through imitation. Copying outfits approached Target buyers offering to sell candles identical to ours for $8.99 instead of our $10 (retail). Some even lodged false complaints about our products, trying to undermine our reputation with Target to create a market niche for themselves. That's the price many companies pay for success.

My partnership with Target withstood such obstacles, as we remained steadfast in our design-leadership business model, leveraging creativity and innovation to drive profitability. For most department stores, the major lever of profitability was, and remains, discount. It's a flawed strategy for increasing profitability and remaining competitive in the long-term. Major retail should operate like Apple and Tesla—those tech companies don't attempt to create the cheapest possible electronics or automobiles. Instead, these design-forward companies occupy coveted niches in the marketplace and sell their products for what they're worth.

But the biggest lessons I derived from Target those first few seasons were personal and cultural. Manufacturers like me and Target managers alike knew how fragile and complicated international supply chains were, and how a typhoon in Japan or an impromptu customs inspection could disrupt even the best and most responsible plans. But Target insisted on transparency and honesty. Right after someone screwed up in the factory, affixing labels incorrectly and thereby delaying our shipment for the week, I needed to communicate with Target immediately. Transparent communication was easy when operations were smooth. It was much more difficult when there were hiccups, like when Typhoon Babs struck the Philippines in October 1998, leaving the cargo ship bearing our merchandize idle as the storm ravaged the island nation.

"Guess what, Jennifer," I said meekly, "the shipment I promised you is several weeks behind schedule."

Making such calls was *extremely* difficult. Jennifer had multiple stakeholders and bosses to whom she was responsible, and my delay impacted them all. I initially worried that such declarations would end the honeymoon phase of my relationship with Target. But my anxiety was more deep-seated than that.

As an Asian, I come from a hierarchy-obsessed cultural context that encourages pleasant and deferential responses when dealing with perceived superiors. In business contexts that entail financial or status inequalities, I'm inclined to divide the world into "us" versus "them." Even when talking to Jennifer that first year, I saw myself as the small vendor pitted against her, the major buyer whose market dominance made her superior to me. I came to understand that this Chinese reflex was embedded throughout my company and its Asian stakeholders. When I initially contacted my sister about this major Target deal, she took a sober look at our industrial operational capacities, and in response to the $1 million order said, "Sure, no problem," despite knowing that this would be highly unlikely, if not impossible.

Over the years, Western companies and contractors have interpreted such cultural instincts as shady or dishonest. In our industry, for example, there are certain textile and glass pigmentations that are difficult to achieve. Many of these are some shade of blue, ranging from the famed lapis lazuli, which costs more than the price of gold, or more recent chemical syntheses like YInMn Blue, patented in 2012 and aesthetically and functionally superior to its cobalt blue cousin.[4] A buyer in Target might fall in love with a particular color like YInMn and seek to have it reproduced in a glass tumbler. But producing it at an industrial scale might prove untenable, because expense and availability might force you to create something similar, but not exact. When confronted with situations like this, my sister and her team were rarely candid and didn't educate buyers about the materials, manufacturing processes, and expenses associated with unique or custom orders. Instead, they chose the less confrontational route, smiling and saying, "No problem." When buyers received the samples, they'd inevitably cry foul. "You told me everything was fine two weeks ago, but this isn't what I ordered. You're such a liar."

To someone coming from a "straight-shooting" Midwestern American context, such "misrepresentation" was dishonest. But my sister's reaction was understandable given her cultural background.

I'd long struggled with this cultural reflex, having created a false sense of peace in my childhood home, and later on, showing quiet deference in my marriage to David and to my bosses at the New York–based medical device company. I'm not casting blame on them, nor am I denying power differentials in the marketplace that unequally structure relationships. My sister needed these contracts, just like I needed my low-paying job in New York. But our cultural upbringing loomed large in these situations, as I simply responded out of humility and fear, thinking that if I said no to others whom I perceived to be more powerful than me, I'd be replaced by someone more eager to say "Yes!"

Target buyers made it clear that my deeply engrained tendency toward dissimulation wouldn't work for them. Their retail operations were premised on accuracy, firm deadlines, and smooth execution. If something went awry, they needed to know immediately so they could make alternative arrangements, redirect the day's shipments, and tweak the planogram to serve their customers. One of the reasons for Target's phenomenal success—which continues to grow in today's otherwise deeply damaged and disrupted retail sector—was that it cultivated and demanded absolute transparency with its stakeholders.

After only one complete retail season, Target's buyers, merchandizers, and managers taught this confrontation-averse Asian not just to communicate, but to *overcommunicate*. And I'm so grateful for it. Despite the deep discomfort it initially caused, honesty proved decisive to my development. It made me stop envisioning the retail world as hierarchically opposed rivals. It began to dawn on me that Target's language of partnership wasn't just corporate rhetoric. Target and I really were partners. Small vendors and Target admittedly occupy vastly different places in the market, but their interests are all aligned, and the success and reputations of all hinge on everyone coming through for one another.

This move to transparency and honesty proved pivotal for me as a businesswoman and a human being. For the first time, I had clarity about my business success. When I'd seen my inventory interspersed throughout Bloomingdale's a few years prior, I'd achieved a symbolic victory. Bed Bath & Beyond and Bloomie's had continually kept me in stock, but their reorders were sporadic, leaving me unclear about how well I was performing. My mind was never at peace; I was always fretting about reorders, all the while wondering if Chesapeake Bay was simply a passing late-twentieth-century fad.

My partnership with Target represented a measurable, transparent victory. Not only had I grown my business about 200 to 300 percent, but I achieved the vaunted status of replenishing vendor. Unlike Bed Bath & Beyond and other box stores where I had previously achieved this title, at Target I joined ranks with Head & Shoulders, Tide, and other everyday essentials. Instead of dreaming of success, or experiencing symbolic victories, I now had quantifiable reports showing my sales numbers and projections with minute transparency. Late in 1998, Richard, David, and I joined other replenishing vendors and Target sales managers at regular forecast meetings, looking at candle department sales reports for the season, reconciling them with the larger planogram projections, and making seasonal forecasts.

Thanks to my work with Target, I developed a growth mindset. Until that point, I'd developed and honed the right hemisphere of my brain by working with people, mastering language, and focusing on design innovation. Excelling at Target required someone fully conversant in logistical operations, advanced supply chain management, and finance. I initially struggled with this because early in life, I'd pigeonholed myself—my sister, Li, was good at math, science, and precision-centered calligraphic arts, while I excelled in language, design, and free-form movement-based arts like dance. As I learned in the late 1990s, I'm actually skilled at number crunching. I began performing balance-sheet, sales forecast, and margin analyses, usurping Richard's position as the "numbers person" in the company. During my team meetings with Target, I began delivering margin assessment and financial projections on the fly, turning the heads of financial analysts.

I turned heads for other reasons during these meetings. My employees in Maryland sometimes made fun of me for what they affectionately termed "Mei-isms." At my Maryland office, I've been quoted as saying, "I wasn't born with a silver platter in my mouth." When faced with an imminent deadline and raw material shortage, I'd shake my head and lament, "This is a real Catch-23." The more I lived in America, the more attuned I became to English aphorisms and expressions. But as David Sunberg has always teased me, they still surface.

One fall day in 1998, during a meeting with Target's upper management, I was speaking of the need to collaborate. *Collaboration* is an overused word in retail, and especially at Target, where it's part of the culture. But instead of saying "collaborate," I said, "Come on, people. Let's calibrate together!"

To my chagrin, David kept kicking me under the table, later shaking his head and chuckling about yet another charming, if embarrassing, Mei-ism.

My ability to synthesize the right and left hemispheres, and my new approach of hyper-transparency, all worked to instill a quiet confidence and maturity within me. Part of that probably arose from working with people at Target, who cheered my success and refused to condescend to me. But it was more than that, as I began to trust my own judgment on the marketplace and follow my own instincts. Richard, a conservative engineer at the company, was often skeptical of my hairbrained design ideas and product-development approaches. It's always great to have an engineer's perspective, especially for a freewheeling creative like me. But I began soberly considering his feedback and making the final decisions on my own, confident in my own capacities.

I began acting similarly with my large vendors. In the coming years, I zealously ensured the quality of my product, and when I received a chargeback letter from Target, indicating a high damage rate for a certain shipment or unscannable bar codes, I ate those costs. I could visualize product breakage from those four-foot distribution box-drops and ink-drained printers and realized I needed to package and label my products better. Whenever the product labels came to us upside down—and this happened several times—I hired a team to unpack and relabel every product. But when retailers were doing poorly and threatened to not reorder my products unless I gave them a massive discount, I didn't automatically oblige them. I'd learned that I wasn't automatically inferior to them, and that I deserved to protect my own interests.

My newfound poise and confidence made me adopt a proactive posture in the marketplace. I'd learned so much about research, marketing, warehousing, and global supply-chain management in the late 1990s, and this knowledge was essential to our operational success. But I knew that for Chesapeake Bay to continue to scale and thrive in the global marketplace, we needed to focus on innovative product development, especially with respect to fragrances. We needed an entire library of fragrance and we needed to scour the world each year, staying abreast of the latest consumer trends, fashions, and art, translating them into the medium of wax. The fate and reputation of this brand rested on design. Beginning in 1998, I resolved to focus on design.

- When growing and scaling your business, seek out strategic partners capable of developing your core strengths and capabilities while also benefiting from and enjoying the advantages you provide.
- Are you hyper-transparent with your partners and stakeholders, or do you default to dissimulation like I initially did? If possible, resist the urge to smile and be accommodating and confront potential obstacles honestly and early. As I learned in my experience with Target, your bottom line and your business relationships benefit from unvarnished honesty.
- Always add value. Reselling operations, like my early company, are destined to be short-term, while entrepreneurial operations, like my design-driven company, add value to the market, constantly innovating based on changing consumer pain points and desires.

Endnotes

1. "Paraffin Wax," *BQ Chemicals*, accessed June 11, 2020, https://www.bqchemicals.com/new/Paraffin-wax.html.
2. "Then & Now: Target's Store Design Philosophy," *Target*, July 31, 2013, https://corporate.target.com/article/2013/07/target-store-design-philosophy-then-and-now.
3. Linda Tischler, "Target Practice," *Fast Company*, August 1, 2004, https://www.fastcompany.com/50058/target-practice.
4. "The Story of YInMn Blue," Oregon State University, accessed May 22, 2020, https://chemistry.oregonstate.edu/content/story-yinmn-blue.

4

FRAGRANCE FORWARD

One weekday morning, sometime in 2013, I interrupted my senior designer, Corina Heymann, who was intently focused on her laptop screen, finalizing some candle-label and product-packaging designs. "Please put your current project away," I asked, "and visit the Fancy Food Show currently underway at the Washington, DC, Convention Center." She shot me a skeptical glance before nodding in agreement.

I'd been confident in Corina's ability to spot diverse consumer trends ever since I'd hired her in April 2006. During our interview, she described how she'd followed her husband to DC and then struggled to find creative work. Corina had focused on print design and product packaging ever since graduating from Virginia Tech in 1990 and had honed these skills in Miami Beach. But she found herself at sea in the nation's capital because most of the jobs were in politics, law, and other noncreative industries. I wasn't surprised. As I used to joke among friends, if you threw a stone at someone in DC, there was a one-in-three chance you'd strike a lawyer and find yourself in deep trouble.

I seized the opportunity to test her creative capacities, taking her on an impromptu field trip to the local Target. We parked, walked to the candle valley, and I pointed to a series of our candles that weren't selling well. "Lean into your creativity," I told her. "Study this product and tell me how I could improve sales."

Corina took the next few days to painstakingly evaluate this poorly selling candle line and reported something insightful to me: the product packaging was overly dominant. Customers couldn't see the candles themselves, she explained, as she furnished some sketches and prototype mockups for a less suffocating product packaging in which the candles themselves took pride of place. That week, I hired her as my senior designer and put her product-packaging solution into place, resulting in more sales.

Like many of my talented designers, Corina had been a boon to the company ever since, and several years later, when I asked her to travel to this culinary show, she'd grown accustomed to my hairbrained and unconventional approach to research and development. She folded up her laptop and headed for the convention center. As she roamed the premises, trying out the free samples and observing the latest in East Coast gastronomy, she noticed one item dominating all others: coconut. Coconut candies, immature coconut water juices, coconut shavings in fruit salads—it was everywhere.

"Coconut is on trend this year," Corina reported during a design team meeting the following week. A few others in the meeting nodded in approval, and after noting that other food companies were working with coconut in some unconventional ways, we began creating "mood boards" filled with current coconut imagery in food, travel offerings, and consumer products like lotion. It was time to translate this into wax, we concluded, and the team sprang into action. We dreamed up a coconut-inspired summer collection, featuring milky-white candles, and worked with our fragrance houses to pair them with just the right scent of this mildly sweet, refreshing tropical staple.

A Random Harvest

Dispatching your senior designer to a food convention might seem bizarre, but it became business as usual at Chesapeake Bay after my snowflake-textured candles propelled us to surprising success at Target. That was when I transformed Chesapeake Bay into a design-focused company. The five elements of candle-making—wax, wick, color, fragrance, and container (or "vessel")—provide endless possibilities for creativity. We innovated over the years in our wax combinations and in the handling of multiple wicks, for example, but these were largely technical and chemically precise considerations. Telling color stories in my candles remained important, and our color palette retained that contemporary, bold, and fresh aesthetic that I'd adopted while roaming the product offerings at the Ambiente trade show and gazing out at Chesapeake Bay in 1995. It was with vessel, and especially with fragrance, that I focused my product innovation.

In 2000, I opened design studios in Rockville, Maryland, and Shanghai, China, staffing them with impressive designers whose specialties ranged from watercolors to digital graphics and photography. My small Maryland team, which began with only two designers, focused on the experimentation phase of the creative process, while my Asia-based team, with designers well versed in Eastern aesthetics, drawing, and oil painting, focused on the production side, executing design blueprints and generating product samples. I was determined to leverage the skills and creativity of this talented group of artists to create a library of diverse fragrances, graphics, and product designs that responded to different seasons, trends, and lifestyles. These designers would travel the world with me—either actually or imaginatively—identifying different cultural moods and trends and seeking design inspiration. Together, I dreamed, we would position this company at the forefront of twenty-first-century lifestyle brands.

As Chesapeake Bay's self-appointed designer in chief, I led by example, setting the tone for what became our unorthodox culture of design. I purchased a cheese grater, applied it to a candle after it solidified, and produced a "linen finish." My team made scaly molds to imitate a crocodile-skin texture, imprinted branches and leaves onto the candle to suggest the outdoors, and created cool feels from the ocean. My intuition led the way: I figured that people love experiencing nature, just like I had on Chesapeake Bay's shores, and would appreciate products that transported them to natural and refreshing settings.

But people also like antique and timeless sensations. We discovered this while visiting green spaces within American, Asian, and European cities, observing the patina-like finishes of aged chairs and buildings, and also at flea markets, seeing the allure of old personal effects, like mercury and silver candleholders. In the early millennium, we reproduced this effect by applying a distressed patina-style finish to glass vessels. Customers loved them.

One day, my design team grew impatient waiting for our wax to cool, and someone threw a sample into cold water. Instead of coming out with Chesapeake Bay's signature snowflake-like texture, it appeared frosted, like icing on a cake. Apparently, the cold water had interacted with the mold's iron metal to create a luscious and smooth ice finish. As I gazed at the candle sample, my thoughts went to consuming Italian ice on a hot summer's day in a Roman or Florentine piazza. That's probably because the cold water frosted the hot metal mold of the candle, muting the colors just enough to convey a feeling of tranquility and refreshment, without sacrificing their vibrancy, which matched the brightness of a summer's day.

Beginning around 2000, I began elevating travel as an essential component of the Chesapeake Bay design process. I can't think of a single company our size that has leveraged travel in its design process as extensively as we did. International trade shows formed the centerpiece of the company's annual travel itinerary. My core group of Maryland-based designers attended the key European shows with me every January and February, where we observed the latest European trends, and we then attended the major American shows in Atlanta and New York, seeing the latest on the American market. Fine fragrance trends begin in Europe and then cross the pond and modify themselves to conform to an American design palette. Frankfurt's annual Ambiente show, which featured the latest in industrial designs, was still my favorite, while

Paris's Maison & Objet, featuring European designers with a focus on natural skincare, bath oils, handmade soaps, and the like, was a close second. Between these shows we also traveled to paper conventions, culinary expos, fashion events, and artistic extravaganzas like Art Basel, further zeroing in on global trends.

During these trips we observed as many materials, fabrics, and colors as possible. Were homemade vessels that year fashioned from glass, ceramic, or metal? What fonts were popular? Was lettering rendered in bright, bold colors or more muted pastels? I converted entire cities into my personal classrooms. I took my team, as well as Target buyers and other stakeholders in later years, to small boutique stores to watch how people told stories through merchandizing, highlighting certain products and fashions.

As I examined the artistry of floral and textile arrangements on the Left Bank of Paris's home interior stores, sampled the intoxicating concoctions from the trendy Marais neighborhood's Palais des Thés, or zigzagged through the souks of Marrakesh, I tried to distill the stories that vendors and merchandizers were curating, or the general mood and spirit of a season or year. No detail was trivial: the paper wrapping chocolates and baguettes in Parisian patisseries, the beautiful calligraphies that accompanied the ice cream cones in London, the striking use of royal purple across the bourgeois boutique industry in Europe, botanical prints in San Francisco's Pacific Heights neighborhoods, and the flower market arrangements in Chelsea's interior design shops in London. Contemporary art, exotic fragrance notes, the latest in luxury, and interior design trends—nothing escaped our notice.

My design team returned to Chesapeake Bay headquarters after each travel season a little exhausted and overwhelmed. It's no wonder; we'd just spent three to seven days engaged in intense trend shopping! But such exposure to diverse global trends also excited us and we always brought nonperishable product samples home with us. We gathered these potions, fabrics, kitsch, and ornaments into what I called the "inspiration library." With these visual aids in hand, we corralled and disciplined our ideas during post-travel meetings, eventually transforming them into product designs.

In 2006, for example, we noticed that throughout the global home décor offerings, black and white was once again on trend, as were minimal and clean-cut designs. We responded with a candle collection called "Classic" that featured solid colors and enduring timeless-looking candle textures. We paired our collection with flat art fonts, executed with minimal lines and no shadows to really capture and convey this idea. Many years later, photography overtook global art. Everyone, it seemed, was trading in painted designs and abstraction for photographic realism—sometimes sharp macrophotography of a blooming flower petal, and sometimes a blurry landscape, with a blade of grass or canoe in hyper-focus in the foreground. We responded in kind with photographs of nature emblazoned on our glass candle vessels.

Around 2000, I instituted Friday "blue sky" trend meetings. These meetings had two rules: nothing was too crazy to discuss, and no topics were off limits. My team indulged me as we discussed everything from reality television shows to dress patterns we'd seen featured on *Project Runway*. It was during this Friday trend meeting that Corina told us about the omnipresence of coconut at the DC food show, after which we began work on coconut-infused white candles.

At another blue sky meeting I described ordering a lychee and rose petal martini one evening after finishing a day of trend shopping in London's stylish Mayfair district and stopping for dinner at the newly opened Hakkasan restaurant. Roses make fabulous fragrances, but the flower itself has always struck me as old-fashioned and lacking a contemporary feel. When roses combine with a fruit, however, the result is juicy and luscious. While drinking the cocktail, I explained to the team, I conceived a whole summer collection of cocktail-inspired fragrances, like lychee rose martini, coconut lime tequila, and raspberry sugar rum. We eventually created a collection of colorful cylindrical "shot glasses" with delicious and tempting fragrances that left you without excess calories or alcohol hangovers. Yet another bestseller.

Of all the wacky topics we discussed during these Friday design meetings, my favorite happened in 2007, following the release of the movie *Perfume: The Story of a Murderer*. I'd adored the story for years as a book, which the secretive and enigmatic Patrick Süskind released to the world in 1985. In eighteenth-century France lived Süskind's fictional Grenouille, the most accomplished olfactory connoisseur and alchemist of scent the world has ever seen. He could detect the subtlest hints of civet, sandalwood, castor, and hop blossom, distinguish them from the more complicated musks of tuberose, cinnamon, jonquil, and jasmine, and creatively combine and distill them all, creating the most complex fragrance library of extracts, salves, pomades, essences, oils, tinctures, and perfume formulas.[1]

After learning the finer points of distillation, Grenouille applied it to leather, grain, glass, porcelain, fresh fish, and human blood, seeing if he could compound an essential oil from them.[2] He refined his techniques to maceration, extracting the "aromatic souls" of metal, wood, doorknobs, and water, and then flies, rats, goats, pigs, and beetles, and even different people.[3]

It might sound farfetched, but this was the olfactory creativity and subtle passion for scent that I wished to inculcate among my designers. As we agreed after the movie screening, it was hard not to walk away enraptured by the power of scent. As Süskind writes:

Odors have a power of persuasion stronger than that of words, appearances, emotions or will. The persuasive power of an odor cannot be fended off, it enters into us like breath into our lungs, it fills us up, imbues us totally. . . . People could close their eyes to greatness, to horrors, to beauty, and their ears to melodies or deceiving words. But they could not escape scent. For scent was a brother of breath. . . . He who rules scent rules the hearts of men.[4]

A Symphony of Fragrance

It was probably inevitable that the next major milestone in my fragrance journey took me and my creative director Carmen Desenne to Grasse, France, still as much the mecca of global perfumery today as it was during Grenouille's fictional exploits in the eighteenth century. In 2006, the Fragrance Foundation invited Carmen and me to join a group of 20–30 industry experts on a pivotal and enlightening trip to the town. Located about an hour and a half outside of Nice, this hub of the global fragrance industry possesses the ideal clayish soil and weather to produce exquisite lavender, bergamot, jasmine, and rose bushes. It's home to specialized agricultural operations like American flavor giant Cargill and Fragonard, as well as hundreds of small vendors, purveying some of the best essential oils and fragrances on the world market.

The region left an immediate impression on me, its old villages reminding me of southern Italy, but its boutique fragrance factories, scattered throughout the countryside, recalling California's Napa and

Sonoma valleys. On the drive from the Nice airport that spring, I reveled in the medieval architecture, the endless fruit trees and trellised vegetable gardens, and the unending rose bushes that released a sweetly intoxicating scent over the region. The entire region seemed to compete for olfactory preeminence, with jasmine, oleander, azalea, lavender, rose, and a variety of citrus notes permeating the surrounding air. It was here that aristocrats and noblemen and women once flocked in search of pleasing scents to mask their body odor and spices to obscure the scent of putrefying meats and energize otherwise bland foodstuffs.

Seeing the landscape in person, I could now appreciate why Grasse became "the Rome of scents," "the promised land of perfumes," and the Paris of pomade since at least the eighteenth century.[5] I could also see why modern haute perfumery thrives there now. Grasse is where the House of Chanel sources and compounds its roses for Chanel N°5, and where Houbigant sources its main ingredients for Quelques Fleurs L'Original, an exclusive and celebrated scent that counted among Princess Diana's longstanding favorites.

As Carmen and I visited cellars, factories, laboratories, and storerooms, I gained a new appreciation for the fragrance industry. Pine is one of the most affordable fragrances on the market and often serves as a base for more complex fragrances. It's one thing to know that abstractly, and quite another to travel to a pine press, as we did, and witness workers operate large metallic machines, guiding pine tree trunks into a series of grinding blades. Within the bowels of the machine, an invisible but noisy industrial process crushed the wood, producing a pile of chip scraps on one side of the machine and a delicate tube of pine oil on the other. At agricultural giant Cargill we watched a cold press extract lemon zest fragrances, and at a company called Mane we saw robotic arms mixing minuscule amounts of expensive, specialized fragrances to a woodsy or citrus base—10 droplets here, 8 there—to create an inimitable and expensive fragrance whose specialized chemistry we couldn't have appreciated until now.

Rose oil production proved an intricate and almost heartbreaking process. For the most expensive oils like these, professional perfumers (what the industry calls "noses") don't render fragrances via extraction, as they do with pine, nor do they cold-press them. Instead, when specialists determine that the roses are at their most fragrant, workers gather millions of beautiful petals and soak them in a soapy mixture, which gradually pulls the fragrance from the petals into the liquid. Workers then transfer the ingredients into a large tank and gently heat them in a vaporization process, allowing oil to separate from the remaining liquids. The heartbreaking part: 10,000 kilograms of flower petals, which could have served as table centerpieces and "just-because" bouquets for hundreds of families or first dates, often yields only 1 kilogram of oil.

This trip was a wakeup call about how much closer and more in touch we needed to be with our fragrance houses. Like a sommelier with wine, a professional nose can detect oak, subtle hints of berries, and minerals, and then chemically recreate them in a laboratory. Like candle-making, perfumery is both art and science, requiring exact chemistry combined with imagination. Prior to this trip, Carmen and I didn't understand this, and we never knew why fragrance prices fluctuated so drastically. We now understood how a $5 or $10 price difference in fragrant oil could vastly change its olfactory sophistication and quality. After this trip, I required everyone in our design and fragrance marketing departments to visit a factory that produced fragrance. We also began training our candle and home-fragrance buyers about fragrances. Without an understanding of compounding and distillation, they sometimes purchased in a vacuum.

Fragrant Storytelling

After our olfactory master's course in Grasse, I was ready to begin storytelling with fragrance. This represented another major milestone for the company. Instead of orienting us within the candle-making business, I began positioning us within the broader home-fragrance industry. Focusing my creativity and innovative capacities on fragrance, I began to notice that every fragrance contained a journey and, if you looked closely enough, told a story of that journey.

Cleopatra told my favorite fragrance story of all time. When this famed queen of Egypt sailed to meet the famous statesman Marc Antony of Rome, she perfumed herself with sandalwood, and infused the boat's atmosphere with exotic Oriental scents of frankincense, myrrh, and cinnamon. When she came to shore in her sweet-smelling boats, she enchanted the Roman general, who gave up his wealth, power, and family for her.[6] Whenever I've tried to tell an intimate or mysterious fragrance story, I draw on Oriental scents of jasmine, musk, and patchouli. Musk and ambers were originally compounded from animal glands, giving them sexual undertones and an intimate and sensual feel. (Luckily all musks are synthetically manufactured now.)

Inspired in part by Cleopatra's ancient fragrance journey, I launched a conceptual fragrance offering called Temple in 2003, which I released in a globally oriented meditation collection. What is the fragrance of a temple? For me, a temple smells like burned redwood incense, a scent I associate with the famous Lingyin Temple in my native Hangzhou and the Buddhist temples of Myanmar. The scent has notes of sandalwood, popular throughout China, India, and Bangladesh, but also notes of dead wood, either accumulating moss and other vegetation on the forest floor or drifting atop rivers or ocean waters. Upon examining these water-logged or abandoned pieces of timber, you'll discover they've almost developed their own distinct fragrance, lending them a magical second life and evoking the divinity that I tried to convey in Temple.

Temple also gestures toward the deep history of perfumery and religious tradition. Before we began adorning ourselves with oils and ointments, they had religious and spiritual significance. Ancient Chinese, Indian, and Egyptian cultures cold pressed floral and botanical fragrances like jasmine and offered them to deities. According to specialists, the world's first perfume came from Cyprus, whose inhabitants burned it as a fragrant offering to Aphrodite.[7] After endearing ourselves to the goddess of love (from whose name derives "aphrodisiac"), we applied scents to our own bodies, trying to endear ourselves to others, especially potential mates.

But what makes Temple significant to me is that it conjures the incense and fragrances of Chinese, Egyptian, and Buddhist mythology just as it does the mindfulness practices currently popular among tech enthusiasts in California's Silicon Valley. Like religion, Temple tells a timeless story. It's the smell of burning wood mixed with rain and fresh blossoms forming on the mountain tops after the winter thaw. Even if you aren't particularly religious like me, the scent still elevates you by connecting you to a divine source.

Every season tells a fragrance story. During a visit to the White House in 2012 to discuss American manufacturing, I asked President Obama what he thought fall's most popular fragrance was. He smiled politely and gave it some thought. "Pumpkin," he replied. I tried to correct the president as gently as I could. It was a solid guess. President Obama naturally thought of this autumnal staple, which we carve at Hallow-een and sometimes sprinkle with sea salt and pepper after roasting in our ovens. But pumpkin itself tells a limited story. Instead, I explained, fall tells the seasonal story of "pumpkin spice." Pumpkin mixed with vanilla and nutmeg is a powerful food and marketing tool as nutmeg is an aphrodisiac, adding spice and zest to an otherwise bland seasonal gourd. At the beginning of the Falliday season, we told pumpkin spice fragrance stories in our candles.

Every person tells a fragrance story, and my journey has given rise to many Chesapeake Bay fragrance combinations. These fragrances speak to my identity as an immigrant who represents a complex blend of Eastern and Western cultural traditions. "Jasmine Water," for example, is a gender-neutral scent that combines the dewy white petals of jasmine with the salty and ozonic drift of crisp morning air on a mid-autumn day wafting across the shores of Chesapeake Bay. In conjuring my two homes of Hangzhou and Maryland, this scent conveys the importance of maintaining a sense of place. If your life journey takes you far from home and around the world, I hope this scent inspires you to carry with you a sense of each place you live or visit.

Lemongrass Eucalyptus is another personal fragrance that conveys my experience of awakening. When energizing lemongrass and verbena gather in the living embrace of invigorating eucalyptus, they combine with notes of lavender and mint to waken the heart, mind, and spirit. Coming to America initially represented such an awakening for me, but as I settled into my job at a medical supply company in New York, I came to discover that American life could be just as mundane and unfulfilling as life had been in China. What mattered wasn't my immediate surroundings and cultural context, but what I chose to do with them. When I light a Lemongrass Eucalyptus candle, I feel invigorated. The notes remind me of my decision to leave my dead-end job and pursue my own version of the American Dream.

I created Oak Moss Amber and Mediterranean Citrus as a reminder to stay rooted when facing challenges in the pursuit of any dream. What better conveys the importance of roots and the passage of time than the mighty oak tree or golden amber? Trees and their life-energizing sap can remain vigorous for centuries, while billions of humans flourish and die. When these scents combine with moss, conveying the oceanic notes of the sea, they suggest the possibility of staying rooted while also exploring other worlds, ideas, and possibilities. The kaleidoscopic notes of Mediterranean Citrus, combining mandarin oranges, grapefruit, cardamom, and bracingly fresh hints of lily, have a similar effect. Its earthier tones of cedar, which has clung to Mediterranean coastlines for centuries, keep us grounded, especially when we feel exciting or destabilizing change, as conveyed by the citrus. Because they embody both past and future, I hope that when people light Oak Moss Amber or Mediterranean Citrus candles, they too can experience the beautiful feeling of rootedness in the soil while simultaneously feeling confidence and freedom to face whatever challenges lie ahead.

Business partners and sisters Li and Mei at the twentieth anniversary celebration of Chesapeake Bay (2014).

Years later, on the twenty-fifth anniversary of Chesapeake Bay (2019), my fragrance team created osmanthus, an olfactory tribute to me and my founding of this fragrance-based candle company. Osmanthus is a tiny flower that blooms in September throughout Japan and China and resembles a grain of rice in a yellow blossom case. A delicate and dry flower, its white floral notes immediately conjure the West Lake district in my hometown of Hangzhou. The striking feature of this flower: the closer you are to it, the less you're able to smell it. But at a distance it permeates the air, and its pleasing aromas can even intoxicate you. I was touched when my creative director presented me with four different sample submissions of the candles from four competing fragrance vendors. Unfortunately, this fragrance never launched, as I retired as CEO in late 2018. But this gesture will forever stay with me, just like the rapturous smell of osmanthus will stay with you if you ever visit Hangzhou's West Lake district in the fall.

Buildings also tell fascinating fragrance stories. Sometimes this is inadvertent, like the deep olfactory signature of an old house or building. Other times it's deliberate. Marketing and merchandizing departments work with fragrance houses to create and infuse fragrance stories into department stores and casinos, usually by diffusing scents through air conditioning vents. Like the origins of perfumery itself, chemists initially designed these building scents to mask odors—body odors and decomposing food in the case of perfumery and spices, and the smell of cigarette smoke for buildings.[8]

But the practice has taken on a positive valence as museums, airports, and other public buildings have begun manufacturing and diffusing "signature scents" to enhance the experience of visiting a building and to cement customer loyalty. Sometimes these scents are seductive. Gramercy Park hotel in New York City, where fashionistas, critics, and editors descend en masse during Fashion Week and other trend-setting occasions, partnered with French fragrance house Le Labo to create Santal 26. After staying at Gramercy Park during a trend-shopping trip in New York, our stylish Target representative David Sunberg began using Santal 26 as his personal fragrance.

The stylish Target rep David Sunberg with Mei at the twentieth anniversary celebration of Chesapeake Bay (2014).

One World Trade Center, which created a signature scent comprised of New York State trees and citrus notes called "One World," faced a much larger challenge with its building's aroma. Its scent has the burden of lending grandeur and respect to this building, constructed on a site where many perished in a terrorist attack, but also extending calm, especially for the many visitors leery of peering out of the glass from the 100th to 102nd floors. Relying on one scent to suggest resilience and inspiration to its visitors is no easy task.[9]

I had no idea about building-based fragrance stories until a trip I made to London during the mid-2000s en route to the Maison & Objet trade show in Paris. Accompanied by a few members of my design team, along with David Sunberg and a few Target buyers, I led everyone through my beloved Harrod's department store, where we leisurely strolled through the different departments until we arrived at the garden department. All of the patrons lingered there almost transfixed. Though it was the dead of winter and London was cold and damp, you wouldn't know it here. Green moss and freshly potted flowers dotted this department, along with lounge chairs and diverse suitcases. The place felt blooming and alive and made me feel like I was lounging at a coastal resort or strolling through a beautiful spring garden. It took me a moment to realize that as visually compelling as the display was, that's not why people were standing motionless and mesmerized.

Using a water-based diffuser, the store was pumping an irresistible aroma of freshly cut grass into the air. At the travel and luggage department, a coconut and Coppertone sunscreen–like fragrance permeated the air as shoppers gathered around the luggage offerings, opening and closing the samples and imagining themselves taking sunbaths on Ibiza. This was the first time I saw fragrance applied as a marketing tool. These scents accomplished what marketers call the "linger-longer factor," motivating consumers to stay put and purchase more items.[10] This also marked the first time I saw scent incorporated into "sensory branding," which refers to correlating sense-related emotional and physiological responses with your product or service. Though this trip didn't inspire a new fragrance story at Chesapeake Bay, it motivated me to approach fragrance-making as a way to elicit emotions, stimulate our imaginations, and transport us to different worlds.

We innovated a little too much at times, resulting in a few fragrance story failures. Remember in the mid-2000s when vegetables grew in prominence as health-obsessed millennials began posting pictures of brussels sprouts and spinach smoothies on social media? Our designers noticed this, too. Vegetables began to experience a cultural moment, with mainstream restaurants trading in steak-and-potato offerings for collard greens and butternut squash risotto, and First Lady Michelle Obama prominently installing a vegetable garden in the White House. But our carrot, kale, and grilled eggplant candles didn't test well and were creative failures.

A state gift Mei designed for First Lady Michelle Obama (ca. 2010).

Sometimes our fragrance flops were culturally rooted. Figs are wonderful fruits that produce understated botanical notes. My European employees regularly brandished a bag of figs and ate them as dessert for lunch. I should have noticed when their American counterparts thought that odd. "Can you eat that without cooking it?" someone once asked during a lunch break. While figs are widespread throughout the northern European, Mediterranean, and Middle Eastern regions, Americans don't snack on them and therefore lack olfactive fig memories. We ultimately discontinued most of the fig fragrances that we designed. Yet when we included figs as a constituent fragrance note but didn't label them as such, they retained their popularity. The same went for lychee fragrances, which are popular in Asia but for which American lack nasal factory memories.

As I worked with my noses and perfume houses to develop these diverse fragrance stories, Chesapeake Bay's library of several hundred fragrances came to assume a distinctive olfactory identity. This marked another breakthrough because in the early years of founding the company, I could only describe this identity in negative terms. As much as I respected the focus and strength of leading American fragrance companies, I didn't want my candles to carry their sweet floral or gourmand palette, which includes such staples as blueberry, raspberry, sugar cookie, and chocolate fudge sundae. But following my experiences in traveling, experimenting, and compounding alongside fragrance houses, we didn't merely veer away from floral and gastronomic notes but matured as a fragrance-based company to have a distinctive essence and identifiable fragrance palette of our own.

I define the olfactory identity of Chesapeake Bay as twofold. Our company was foremost distinguished by its environmental fragrances inspired by nature. Specifically, we gravitated to botanical, ozonic, and green notes (instead of floral) that smelled of pine, natural landscapes, and masculine colognes. Secondly, our olfactory identity veered toward the conceptual. What is the smell of waking up? What is the smell of happiness? These questions might seem silly to everyone but Grenouille, because feelings are highly subjective and cultural—what makes one person happy might make another morose. But conceptual fragrances have found a market. In 1997, Clinique made a major milestone in the area when it debuted its bright orange Happy. The popularity and professional acclaim of this fragrance suggests that there is an emerging consensus: happiness smells a lot like mimosa, bergamot, and grapefruit.[11]

There's a science to fragrance (discussed below), and certain universals can enable fragrance makers to evoke landscapes and describe abstract concepts. Cinnamon, for example, is a stimulating fragrance that arouses people, while chamomile and lavender are relaxing fragrances that might evoke joy and contentment but are too mellow to inspire happiness and excitement. Working within universal parameters, my fragrance notes aspired to achieve the excellence and sophistication of French designer Hermès. Some of the world's most advanced noses work at this storied French design and luxury house, and they've assembled a world-class collection of conceptual and non-floral environmental notes. My complex fragrances, like my musk-infused Copper Moon, simultaneously veer toward the conceptual, contemporary, and environmental. Like Hermès's, Chesapeake Bay's designers never reported to marketing departments, making them beholden to their imaginations instead of balance sheets and focus groups.

Relishing this freedom, chemist and Hermès in-house perfumer Christine Nagel describes her approach to perfumery as that of a ballerina whose years of practice and discipline are apparent in every arabesque; as that of a painter, drawing on a palette of materials to forge new scent canvases; and even as that of a wanderer on a spiritual quest.[12] I tried to muster that same imagination to conceive of my Full Moon fragrance, thinking about what color the full moon might be (I landed on purple), how to capture the artistic celebrations and debauchery that characterize the full moon in ancient and contemporary lore (infusing it with a sensuous Oriental musk), and how to evoke the ambiance of the foreign environment (adding a hint of wisteria, suggesting the smell and texture of lava rocks).

Like all great libraries, my fragrance collection had an essence but also contained paradoxes and even contradictions. Chesapeake Bay's fragrance library was sophisticated yet accessible, complex yet refreshingly simple, highly abstract and precise, playful and philosophical, and warm and edgy. It contained European elegance, the grandeur of American landscapes like Chesapeake Bay, and the magic and majesty of the Orient. It was simultaneously on-trend and timeless.

Fragrance Delivery

Chesapeake Bay's signature fragrances, which came to center on environmental and conceptual notes, were predominantly diffused through refined petroleum wax. When I started the company in 1995, we were a pillar-candle operation, providing stand-alone wax candles ("pillars") of staggered widths and heights and of different colors. These were the candles I had originally experimented with in Campbell's soup cans and later saw interspersed throughout Bloomingdale's in lime green and white. But as I innovated more with fragrances, we broadened our vessels accordingly, and by 1999, we started using glass and ceramics to hold our fragrance-infused candles. This was our first major vessel variation, and I immediately experimented with different color and texture combinations, applying an acid wash to create a "frosted" look and working with glass manufacturers to make colored and crisply clear finishes. Despite the aesthetic appeal of frosted glass, particularly in different colors, it was rare to see it in most cosmetic and candle products, simply because of the expense. We made candles, but not glasses, and had to collaborate with glass manufacturers, who either provided us something "texture-forward" or furnished us simple vessels to which we added texture, color, and silk-screening in the factory.

By the turn of the millennium we had transformed ourselves from a predominantly pillar-making brand into a jar-candle outfit. Some of this was texture-driven, and we wanted to add more style and elegance to home décor items that often featured a plain glass jar paired with one fragrance. I thought about the contemporary and minimalist homes throughout America and used that as a lens and design perspective to create more fashionable offerings. I also experimented with alternative materials like tins, bamboo, and concrete. Focusing on jars instead of pillars conferred major fragrance advantages. One pillar candle can only contain 4 percent fragrances—anything more and the candle destabilizes and begins sweating or bleeding excess fragrances as it burns. Jar candles, by contrast, hold significantly more fragrance.

Whether they come in glass vessels or stand-alone pillars, candles are optimal fragrance delivery systems because of the heat they deliver. But candle fire carries major safety risks. I've always shuddered to think about children or pets colliding with open flames and injuring themselves, or of an unattended candle setting a house ablaze in a fire-prone region like California. These fears crystallized in 2000, during a focus group that Target hosted in Atlanta. At the meeting, we asked consumers about their candle-purchasing decisions and larger lifestyle habits. I'll never forget one of the ladies fawning over my candles.

"I love Chesapeake candles so much!" she gushed. "I burn them all day long! My favorite is lighting some candles before I leave for the grocery store. When I return home, the house smells just wonderful!"

I froze and felt a searing pain in my chest. Our candles always came with warning labels strongly urging people never to leave their burning candles unattended. And here was a well-meaning and satisfied customer blissfully violating this rule.

While continuing my innovation in wax, my interests and safety concerns inspired me to pursue nonflammable home-fragrance products. I wanted my products to add refinement and luxury to a home space without creating mortal risks. As I began surveying the market, I saw plenty of alternative fragrance-releasing products, including incense (which didn't entirely eliminate the fire threat), scented caviar beads, and a variety of perfumed sprays used to remove the pesky odors of a teenage boy's gym bag, kitty litter, and the like. I wanted to create something more innovative than these product offerings, so I experimented with wood beads and shredded wood chips, finding cork and other light trees to be strong fragrance conveyers. Unfortunately, the balls and chips became stained, greasy, and unattractive after several uses and I abandoned the idea.

In addition to safety and creativity, my interest in developing fragrance delivery rested on a new market trend called fragrance layering. The concept is easy enough. If you really like Chanel N°5, you probably won't object to extending your enjoyment of the fragrance beyond the famous perfume or eau de toilette. You'll probably want to buy Chanel N°5 hand soaps, bath lotions, candles, and the like. American soap and lotion chain Bath & Body Works led the market in this trend. Walk into any one of their stores and you'll likely find fragrances delivered in as many as 40 formats. If you like vanilla, you could choose from hand lotions, soaps, bath bombs, candles, and tea-light diffusers. By varying my delivery vessels, I could diversify my offerings, introducing novel and safe ways to express my fragrances.

Every year in the new millennium, I challenged my team to produce one major fragrance-delivery innovation, and our first one was a hit. During one of my design trips through Europe, I noticed companies working with sticks derived from certain reed grasses found along riverbanks throughout South Asia. Companies doing R&D work just like me probably went scavenging along Asian riverbeds, plucking blades of grass from the banks and removing the fibrous skins to find a delicate stick with many pores remaining. Once treated and dried to prevent molding, these delicate sticks proved efficient fragrance diffusers.

I had visions of doing for reed diffusers what I'd done for my Target candles—bringing high-end products, which were only available at expensive boutiques and department stores, to a more mainstream American market. I began scouring for materials in China, looking to find reeds that could absorb and diffuse fragrances. Though I wasn't the first to conceive of reeds as great fragrance diffusers, I wondered if I might be the first market entrant in the United States. At the time, I was competing against Zodax, a design-focused home-fragrance company like mine, which emerged as my archrival at Target. We began experimenting with alcohol-based fragrance formulas. Alcohol is a convenient vehicle for transporting fragrance into the air, but we faced so many regulatory obstacles that we abandoned it. For over a year we worked on the chemistry of the fragrance, experimenting with water-based solutions and continually failing.

Preparing the best grasses also posed a major challenge. Sometimes we ordered reeds that arrived to us encased in mold! The grasses were either poorly treated or external moisture had seeped into the packaging. At other times, our products shipped from Asia during monsoon season, creating mold infestations throughout the entire shipping container. No matter how it happened, finding moldy reeds was like smelling notes of gasoline in our petroleum wax—a nightmare. Have you ever purchased asparagus in the grocery store, or even a box of candies and chocolates, and found a white Styrofoam-like strip between the product and its lower packaging? That little strip is a drying agent, present to capture any excess moisture to prevent product despoliation. After several toxic shipments of reeds came our way, we found conscientious vendors in East Asia who properly dried and treated their reeds and shipped them with drying agents.

Delivering diffusers to market proved yet another obstacle. Even if you had great reeds and chemically stable fragrances suitable for dispersing scents with them, the product assembly carried some risk. Sometimes our fragrance oils leaked, just like a shampoo bottle might. In addition, the glasses, sealed reeds, and fragrances had to be protected and properly assembled in a box, something that a machine couldn't accomplish. This was a labor-intensive process, and we had to deliver at higher volumes and lower price points to our Target and Bed Bath & Beyond customer channels. Box store patrons aren't accustomed to spending over $30 for anything, so we had to deliver these complex boutique-quality packages at low prices.

We ultimately beat Zodax and our other competitors as the first company to introduce reed diffusers to a mainstream American market. But even this was and remains a mixed blessing. During product test meetings, people thought they were supposed to burn the reeds (defeating the entire purpose). And one day while entertaining my friends and their young twins in 2014, one of them made their way into my first-floor powder room. We heard a child's scream, rushed to the scene, and found that the young boy had consumed the contents of the reed diffuser. We took him to the emergency room. He was unharmed, but I still shudder at the memory.

Despite the obstacles, the reed diffuser that we debuted in the mid-2000s was our first successful fragrance-delivery innovation. Though we'd introduced incense in one of our earlier collections, Americans weren't accustomed to burning it, and it never took off. The reed diffusers, by contrast, continually drove business volume. We didn't introduce the reed diffuser as a stand-alone endcap offering, but instead included it alongside our candles. In this way, reed diffusers not only expanded our fragrance delivery options, but represented our first success in fragrance layering.

In keeping with Chesapeake Bay's love of nature, I also sought more "natural" fragrance-delivery systems. We partnered with a vendor in China to create a humidifier: a small machine that used ultrasound technology to power fragrance-diffusion. You simply poured water in a plastic basin, along with some drops of fragrance, and the system released a refreshingly scented vapor into the air. Released in 2015, this product was safe, easy to use, and ideal for multiple climates. In the summer seasons, rather than lighting a candle, you might prefer a cool, refreshing mist. In the dry winter, customers flocked to the product as well, as it diffused scent and humidified simultaneously.

In my fragrance fantasies, I've always dreamed of creating a mobile device called "Mei's Pod." Imagine a device resembling an iPhone that receives infused fragrance cartridges. At the flick of a switch, the machine disperses scents like lavender or sandalwood into the surrounding environment. Have you ever found yourself in a New York City taxicab or Uber, with the scents of garlic and sweat wafting over you, or have you ever walked into a baby nursery or garage and wished to banish the smell you encountered? Mei's Pod is an ideal solution. In the post-COVID world, I also envision that these fragrance cocoons would help keep us safe during travel, with cartridge chips containing deodorizers, decontaminants, and antimicrobial agents that could make an airplane or train seat more pleasant and healthy.

The reason Mei's Pod doesn't yet exist is because this ambitious fragrance-delivery system relies on the same future technological innovations that electric car designers eagerly await. At the time I'm writing this book, an electric car battery can last for 350 miles at most. Whoever powers innovation in electrical battery longevity, allowing vehicles to travel 500, 1,000, and eventually cross-country on a single charge, will revolutionize personal travel. And there will be other beneficiaries of that technology because those batteries will hopefully provide the power needed to heat and deliver pleasant and natural scents into the environment.

A Legacy of Fragrance

In addition to enlivening our environments at home and possibly during travel, I've also dreamed of using the environmental fragrances that I helped pioneer at Chesapeake Bay to improve human health. I've been interested in the therapeutic applications of fragrance ever since I learned about the science of aromatherapy. Upon meeting Peter French and beginning my fragrance journey with the company, I explored different fragrance houses throughout the world, learning about their diverse focuses and strengths as well as the research and development initiatives they undertook. My journey took me to International Flavors & Fragrances (IFF), one of the world's largest fragrance houses based in New York and with laboratories and compounding facilities in New Jersey.

My contact at IFF was a European who gravitated to my contemporary and clean aesthetic. One day in late 1996, he took me on a tour of the facilities and introduced me to a few of the company's in-house noses. One was an Indian man around 90 years old who introduced me to the science of aromatherapy. Certain fragrances, he explained to me, represent powerful stimulants that impact our emotional response system and promote human wellness and well-being.

On a piece of paper, the Indian fragrance expert drew a graph with a horizontal x-axis and a vertical y-axis. The x-axis represented emotion, with one pole indicating "happiness," and the opposite labeled "depression." The y-axis was defined at the top with "alert/active" and at the bottom with "passive/sleep." The entire graph yielded four quadrants and every single fragrance in the world, this nose told me, lives somewhere in these four quadrants.

A fragrance can be happy and produce a slightly sedate effect, or it could live at the high end of alert but still be sad. Consider the lemon. Its scent is one of happiness and alertness and lives in the upper-right quadrant. Don't you feel refreshed and happy on a summer day when you guzzle a glass of lemonade? Cinnamon, by contrast, doesn't make you happy, so it is somewhere in the middle of that axis, but it definitely wakes you up and stimulates your other senses. The tropical Asian ylang-ylang flower, he explained, belongs somewhere nearer to lavender on the graph, given that its antidepressant and antianxiety properties create happiness but its ability to control heartbeat and fight insomnia gives it a relaxing feel.

This meeting left an impression on me. Though I never formally introduced the graph at the company, I've always kept it in mind when evaluating fragrances. I've found it especially helpful when developing highly conceptual fragrances, as it has given me a baseline for how to evaluate a certain scent's effect on our emotions. Moreover, this introduction prompted me to explore the science of aromatherapy. Practitioners of traditional medicine in China, Japan, and India have used aromatherapy for centuries, harnessing its antibacterial and antiviral properties to alleviate the pain of pregnancy and to fight insomnia, cancer, and cardiovascular disease.[13] Some Western medical practitioners are convinced of the powers of aromatherapy, while others remain dubious, believing it all operates on the power of suggestion. In other words, you might think that the lavender mist you spray on your pillow helps you sleep, and due to a fragrant "placebo effect," it just might!

Scientific consensus is starting to lead in a pro-aromatherapy direction, revealing how powerful environmental priming can be to reversing the aging process. My interest in this research was piqued in 2014 when the *New York Times* published a spread in its magazine on the pioneering work of Harvard psychology professor Ellen Langer. In her 1981 counterclockwise study, Langer transported eight elderly men, suffering the wear-and-tear of aging, back to their youth in the late 1950s.[14] This was an immersive, multiday, role-playing experience, in which Langer left Cold War news coverage of the time scattered about the place, played Ed Sullivan television programs, and even treated the men like they were younger, telling them to cart their luggage up the stairs themselves. Because they had been psychologically primed to experience a more youthful moment in their personal histories, these men started to look and behave in a younger fashion. After only five days, all of their biomarkers markedly improved.

Langer's important work over the decades, which has replicated and expanded these general findings, has helped to overturn a mistaken medical premise: that we only get sick because a virus or bacterial agent infects us. Instead, she's revealed how environmental factors can both contribute to aging and also jumpstart our own healing. As I read and explored this research, I couldn't help but think about how the application of scent could enliven this research, given its power to awaken the senses and evoke submerged memories that we can no longer access.

I dream of one day partnering with a scientist or biomedical startup to develop a series of environmental fragrances that could awaken memories within people suffering from Alzheimer's disease, Parkinson's disease, dementia, and other forms of neurodegeneration. Olfaction is the most underutilized of our five senses, and it deserves some attention in this therapeutic space. Sight is the longstanding king of the senses, as visually based media like video reign supreme, while auditory media form a close second, as we're constantly bombarded with music and other sounds. We have increasingly well-developed taste palettes. With millennials valuing experiences over possessions, dining and gastronomic experiences have led to a major increase in restaurant culture and specialized cuisine. Our sense of touch is also on point, and if we extend our hands, we can immediately sense the different textures of cotton, leather, and gelatin—these sensations might even stir emotions.

But scent is something far more detailed, powerful, and complex. The nerves involved with olfaction directly connect to those linked with memory. That's why smell often evokes memories of our childhood: our mother's perfume, our grandmother's cake, or our grandfather's musky leather suitcase. But in our era of what one commentator has called "ocular overload," scent remains the most underdeveloped of the five senses. Companies have taken note, seeing their sales and brand loyalty increase after making the "signature scents" I described above part of their marketing and branding efforts.[15] Medical science has similarly taken notice: "The quickest way to change mood or behavior is with smell," said Dr. Alan R. Hirsch, the neurological director of the Smell and Taste Treatment and Research Foundation in Chicago.[16] As Hirsch describes, research on the topic has shown that baked goodies like cookies awaken childhood memories, while floral fragrances improve learning rates. And several scientific studies have tested the effect of aromatherapies on neurodegeneration, with one concluding that the researchers "found aromatherapy an efficacious non-pharmacological therapy for dementia. Aromatherapy may have some potential for improving cognitive function, especially in AD (Alzheimer's Disease) patients."[17]

I envision a future of fragrance. Just like our era of mass customization has personalized everything from our own gloves, ties, and watches to medicines, I believe people, much like buildings, will all soon have personalized signature scents. My dream is to expand those scents so that they heal us instead of simply serving as extensions of our personalities. I sometimes wonder: What if I had been able to engineer a scent from my dad's childhood that could have awakened some of his memories? What if, upon experiencing that scent, we could have reminisced about the factory in China and other fond memories from our time in Hangzhou?

Partnering with scientists and chemists, I'd like to begin with modest olfactory experiments. We'll inject senior living facilities with bursts of cinnamon, lemon, and orange citrus notes in the morning, observing whether this stimulates and energizes the occupants for the day ahead, and do the same with chamomile and lavender in the evening, observing whether they have a relaxing effect. I'd then like to personalize these scents for patients suffering from terrible diseases like my father did, and compound personalized scents from their youth to bring submerged memories to consciousness. We already understand the power of fragrance to awaken nostalgia, increase spending, and—hopefully as a result of Chesapeake Bay—add texture, vibrance, and energy to a living space. I now dream of leaving a fragrant legacy of wellness and healing to the world as well.

- Innovation doesn't just refer to smartphone applications and computer chips. I built a company around fragrance innovation and its many delivery mechanisms.
- Do your products or services pose bodily harm or entail environmental risk? If so, seize this as an opportunity to innovate. After I began worrying about fires, I started thinking beyond my core product of candles to safer and profitable fragrance-delivery vessels. This enhanced my brand and bottom line, all the while promoting increased safety.
- When starting a new business, identify something missing in the market. In the competitive fragrance industry, I found companies focusing on packaging, celebrity marketing, and "gourmand" (food-based) scent palettes. I therefore pivoted to more botanical and imaginative fragrance combinations.
- Your innovations might have unforeseen applications. Who could have imagined that a scent, created to infuse candle wax, might one day have aromatherapeutic applications, helping cure diseases and improve lives? Persevere when your business becomes difficult and the market competitive, because your products and services might one day yield such results, too.

Endnotes

1. Patrick Süskind, *Perfume: The Story of a Murderer* (Vintage International: New York, 1986), 36–37.
2. Ibid., 98–99.
3. Ibid., 184–187.
4. Ibid., 82, 155.
5. Ibid., 166.
6. Tilar J. Mazzeo, *The Secret History of Chanel No. 5* (New York: Harper, 2011), 40; "A Perfumed Affair," *Clive Christian*, accessed July 7, 2020, https://www.clivechristian.com/cleopatra-perfumed-affair/.
7. Mazzeo, *The Secret History of Chanel No. 5*, 19.
8. James Barron, "That Smell at the Top of One World Trade? It's on Purpose," *New York Times*, August 7, 2019, https://www.nytimes.com/2019/08/07/nyregion/wtc-observatory-smell-scent.html.
9. Ibid.
10. Ibid.
11. Liana Satenstein, "How Clinique Happy Engineered My Happiness," *Vogue*, October 31, 2019, https://www.vogue.com/article/clinique-happy-effect-perfume-history.
12. Annie Brown, "How Hermès First Female Perfumer Broke into the Boys' Club," *Financial Review*, December 9, 2019, https://www.afr.com/life-and-luxury/fashion-and-style/how-herm-s-first-female-perfumer-broke-into-the-boys-club-20191205-p53h2g.
13. Babar Ali, "Essential Oils Used in Aromatherapy: A Systemic Review," *Asian Pacific Journal of Tropical Biomedicine* 5, no. 8 (August 2015), https://doi.org/10.1016/j.apjtb.2015.05.007.
14. Bruce Grierson, "What if Age Is Nothing but a Mind-Set?" *New York Times Magazine*, October 22, 2014, https://www.nytimes.com/2014/10/26/magazine/what-if-age-is-nothing-but-a-mind-set.html.
15. Steve Harvey, "Sensory Branding Strategies to Seduce your Customer's Senses," *Fabrik*, February 27, 2019, https://fabrikbrands.com/sensory-branding/.
16. Barron, "That Smell at the Top of One World."
17. Daiki Jimbo et al., "Effect of Aromatherapy on Patients with Alzheimer's Disease," *Psychogeriatrics* 9, no. 4 (December 2009): 173–179, https://doi.org/10.1111/j.1479-8301.2009.00299.x.

5

MADE
IN AMERICA

As I've always joked, candles are like condoms: they're recession-proof. The Asian financial crisis (1997), dot.com bubble, post-9/11 recession, Great Recession (2007–2009), and the COVID-19 pandemic devastated countless industries. But candle sales only surged. When travel, jewelry, or other high-end consumables prove too expensive, consumers turn to candles as affordable and attractive luxuries.

Rather than global downturns, our existential threat arrived in the early 2000s and took the form of antidumping tariffs. Many countries impose these duties on certain companies or product categories to ensure that these imports compete fairly with their domestic rivals. America is no exception. If one bad actor "dumps" products in the American market at unfairly low prices, domestic competitors can petition the Department of Commerce to initiate antidumping reviews.

As a non-market economy whose exports had increased exponentially in the 1990s and early 2000s, China was subject to especially stringent antidumping rules. If one Chinese company dumped products like candles into the U.S. market, antidumping rules issued against those factories applied to everyone in the industry, regardless of whether they had actually dumped products.

Antidumping duties had always been a business reality for our company, and each year they cut deeper into our profit margins. As I saw these tariffs mount around 2000, I had a sneaking suspicion they might destroy the Chinese candle export industry. I was right. In 2004 the antidumping duty on all Chinese candle imports to the United States surged from 58 percent to over 150 percent! Making a profit by shipping candles from China to America was no longer possible.

Around 2002, David and I had begun scouring the world for alternative places to manufacture our products. We began in Tijuana, a town separating Mexico's Baja California peninsula from the American city of San Diego. The city is notorious for its drug traffic and violence, and after visiting a few industrial parks, we understood why and began looking elsewhere. We visited the Philippines, a beautiful country where former U.S. air force bases now serve as bustling commercial industrial zones. Upon arriving, however, we were saddened to find widespread public unrest and armed soldiers guarding our potential warehouses. Thailand, our next location, was better, but while we enjoyed the kind hospitality of our hosts, labor costs here ran higher than in other Asian countries, and the hot weather made it an unattractive location for candle manufacturing.

My ability to spot a trend certainly helped lead us to Vietnam. Implacable foes during the Cold War, the Vietnamese and American governments normalized diplomatic relations in 1995, enabling Vietnam's traditionally agrarian economy to industrialize. I took an immediate liking to this newly opened country when I visited in 2002. Vietnam offered a striking mixture of Eastern and Western influences. Cows roamed the streets, interrupting traffic along bumpy dirt road corridors as workers sporting iconic triangular hats peacefully tilled the beautiful rice patties in the distance. French colonial influences permeated the country, with baguette venders, Western iced coffee, and marvelous French-Vietnamese fusion cuisine at every urban street corner. But I was most taken with the country's attractive business climate. With a young, educated, and hardworking workforce, Vietnam reminded David and me of China in the 1980s. Almost half of the corporate managers we met spoke Mandarin Chinese, while the Buddhist architecture reminded me of my natal Hangzhou.

The labor costs, language, and industrious workforce won us over, and in 2004 we moved our manufacturing operations to the northern Vietnamese city of Hanoi. Proud that we'd manufacture products for export to the United States on its soil, the local government gave us an advantageous price for an industrial park and eased importation costs for our source ingredients coming from China. Establishing and scaling our Vietnamese operations proved seamless; we hired 500 new workers that first year, staggering them into two rotating shifts, and eventually grew to 3,000 employees in all, the same number we had at the peak of our Chinese operations.

Aroma Bay Candle, as we called our new factory, was Vietnam's first candle manufacturer, and when our competitors took note, many followed suit. After several years our small northern Vietnamese region formed a miniature candle industry, with five or six operations releasing intoxicating fragrances into the local atmosphere. Despite the country's underdeveloped infrastructure and increasing competition, Vietnam did more than save us from the existential threat of antidumping. It allowed us to thrive.

Candles on the assembly line in Vietnam (2020).

Vietnamese Victory

Most of all, our Vietnamese operations fueled our innovation. I've always believed that design and manufacturing belong together, and that controlling manufacturing enables innovation. While most of my rivals outsourced manufacturing and competed on product pricing, I leveraged manufacturing to focus on currying favor among consumers with my designs.

Beginning in Vietnam, my designers began experimenting with tin, glass, cement, and ceramic vessels. My company wasn't the first to use unique jar vessels to house candle wax, but we were the first to render them as luxury and fashion items, thanks to my company's experimentation with textures and our infusion of highly innovative fragrances into our wax. Think of the company's Chinese-made pillar candles as representing fashion basics, like blue jeans and a white shirt, while these Vietnamese-produced jar candles were my couture dress or chic office ensemble, designed to perform.

This fashion-driven jar-candle business took off in Vietnam, and we began creating specialized collections for major retailers like Kohl's, Bed Bath & Beyond, and, of course, Target. In 2007, for example, I created a highly popular jar-candle line for Kohl's under a "private label," or store-owned brand, called "Sonoma." Based on Sonoma's success, I recommended a Chesapeake Bay exclusive collection to Target called "Home Scents," a fragrance-driven collection that produced record sales volumes.

My most significant Vietnamese product innovation was the high-fragrance box candle. During one of my annual R&D voyages to London in the mid-2000s I visited a Jo Malone boutique. Jo Malone began in the mid-1990s as a beautician in London, right around the time I began experimenting with wax in my Maryland basement. I learned of her because we shared a similar aesthetic, gravitating to botanical mixtures and refusing to compromise on purity and quality. In 1999, Estée Lauder purchased Jo Malone, giving the small boutique, acclaimed for its quality fragrances, a global distribution.

During that visit, Jo Malone's candles, housed inside elegant boxes, spoke to me. I'd noticed such box-candle offerings throughout European department stores and high-end boutiques elsewhere on that trip and wondered if Americans had not caught the trend because of the steep prices. My mind then went to the reed diffusers I'd seen in Italy during another R&D trip (see Chapter 4). Perhaps I could democratize these upscale candle offerings and make them available to a mainstream consumer base, just like I had with the reeds.

Shortly after we began manufacturing in Vietnam, I sensed that American consumers might gravitate to such an offering and worked with my senior designers to introduce high-fragrance box candles to Target. My challenge was considerable. I needed to sell a premium fragranced candle, just like those on offer at the cosmetic counter of Bloomingdale's or Neiman Marcus, at $9.99 instead of $50–$75. Delivering a Jo Malone value proposition at a Target price point proved difficult because of our quality standards. We sourced our ingredients from fragrance vendors similar to those used by Chanel, Tom Ford, and Jo Malone. The top notes of these high-end producers might contain more essential oils than ours, but the quality was comparable.

But Jo Malone sourced its handmade candles and boxes in London and sold its products at the cosmetic counters of Neiman Marcus, Bloomingdale's, and Saks Fifth Avenue, elevating the company's marketing costs and decreasing its margins. Saving on marketing and enjoying higher volumes proved major pricing variables for us, as we ordered wax, packaging, and essential oils at lower costs, all the while avoiding antidumping tariffs entirely. And the product packaging was important. I found that if you added a box to a candle, you could double the price—all the while using it to preserve even more innovative fragrances.

During my trips to New York, Paris, and elsewhere, I searched for innovative items to fill these boxes. As always, I gravitated to minimalist styles with contemporary and modern points of view and used natural botanical fragrances to achieve balance and harmony in these collections. Pure & Natural, an aesthetically minimalist and botanically fragranced collection, was one of our more successful box-candle offerings. Like all of our collections, it was design-driven and anchored with an assortment of fragrances that represented the line's soul—only this time, consumers took it home in a lush box.

Target launched our box candles in May 2006 as a seasonal endcap program. The popularity of these box sets, combined with the quality of our Vietnamese-manufactured candles, was so impressive that in late 2006 Target gave us an extra 16 feet at 1,000 stores for an innovative "high fragrance" program. (By comparison, I only had another 8 feet for all of my other collections.) This extra real estate housed our box collections along with a new high-fragrance-load jar candle. We doubled our fragrance load in these new candles and customers loved them, continually requiring us to restock this vast 16 feet in Target's candle valley.

But even as fragrance-driven box collections and stand-alone jar candles drove business volumes, our Vietnamese operations began to suffer around the time of the Great Recession in 2008. As the U.S. economy began to exhibit signs of weakness, commodity prices soared, drastically increasing our air and ocean shipment costs. Our Chinese wax, glasses, bamboo lids, labels, and fragrances became excruciatingly expensive, as did shipping our finished products into American ports. When the global economy began contracting, moreover, overseas shipping companies began decreasing their routes, imperiling our company's turnaround and "time to market."

Labor costs also soared. Because antidumping had propelled many industries to relocate to Vietnam, wages and salaries began swelling there. When we established industrial operations in northern Vietnam,

Hai Phong, where we shipped our candles, was a quaint port, with several Japanese-owned TV manufacturers and a few other electronic companies regularly doing business there. Over the next few years, toy companies, furniture makers, and fashion outfits all moved in and the output grew so vast that they all had to stagger production so that their manufacturing facilities could remain continuously open. Due to simple supply and demand, not to mention the relatively small size of Vietnam's population, demand for local workers skyrocketed and from 2006 to 2009 our factory salaries increased around 30 percent.

Chesapeake Bay had largely created the fragrant candle industry in Asia, and our competitors wanted in so badly that they offered to pay our workers to steal fragrance samples. These formulas were just as valuable to our company as a hard-won drug patent for a pharmaceutical corporation, a copyright to a motion picture company, or a proprietary algorithm for a Silicon Valley powerhouse.

With skyrocketing costs and cutthroat competition, I needed to leverage the goodwill I'd garnered over the years to negotiate price increases with our main retail customers. Bad timing—our major retailers were in the throes of the global financial crisis. Instead of entertaining price increases, they sought discounts on my products and requested that I shoulder more responsibility for warehousing, asking me to store finished products so that they could lower their inventory-management costs. Just like antidumping, these challenges were staggering.

A possible solution only crystallized one day in 2008 during a routine conversation I had with a senior buyer. It was a pleasant and enjoyable exchange, especially at first. This buyer informed me of how well the Home Scent collection was selling, and we discussed consumer trends. Pillar candles, we noted, were popular as decorative items, like throw pillows on a day bed, and told a color story in many American homes. Purple candles might showcase spring while two pink pillars in a bathroom might exude femininity and soft elegance. But because jar candles didn't require external holders and held so much fragrance, their use rate was much higher. For every pillar candle we sold, the buyer informed me, consumers purchased 5–6 jars. My Vietnamese-manufactured jars outsold our pillars by so much that most of my major retailers continuously sold out their stock and many provided dedicated real estate just for the Home Scent collection. I couldn't help but agree, as these jar candles represented some of my most technically mature work to date.

Despite our quality and competitiveness with consumers, however, one of my major retail buyers asked for a discount on upcoming orders. Given the increased costs of business, I had to decline. Facing an impasse, the buyer casually said, "You might want to consider manufacturing in the United States."

It was the first time someone broached the idea. Maryland always served as the creative and spiritual capital of Chesapeake Bay candles, its beautiful shores providing the inspiration for my environmentally based and contemporary aesthetic. But transferring manufacturing there had never seemed feasible. Though candles were one of the few industries that America hadn't outsourced, most domestic candle factories were fully automated. Although I'd begun the automation of certain industrial processes in China and accelerated those trends in Vietnam, my design-driven and fragrance-forward manufacturing operations were much less automated than my American counterparts'. It didn't seem like a good fit.

Prohibitive labor costs were the biggest deterrent. Following the global recession, certain manufacturers had begun reshoring operations to America, but this was far from a mass movement. For the majority of industries and product categories, foreign manufacturing was still most cost-effective. In 2009, I began soul searching. Could I possibly relocate manufacturing again, this time not within Asia, but to the United States?

Burned in Maryland

Recognizing the many logistical, financial, and even cultural complexities of U.S. manufacturing, David and Richard, my two hard-nosed engineers, expressed strong skepticism. Richard loved Vietnam because it had zero antidumping costs, affordable facilities, and a young, skilled, hardworking, and relatively inexpensive labor force. I knew I couldn't convince him of my dream, born of design leadership: bringing the brand to Maryland so that I could leverage design and manufacturing to power innovation. No matter how I framed it, we all knew that American manufacturing would cost us millions and represented a huge risk. In hindsight, I'm glad I didn't know how expensive, harrowing, and soul-crushing it would actually be. Otherwise, I might have never done it.

Despite the protestations of my senior team, I began surveying the country for manufacturing facilities for rent or purchase in 2009.

We needed a site near a major port because much of our raw materials like glass arrived from China. California had strong appeal especially since we'd had a third-party warehouse in Long Beach since 1998. Despite its proximity to major ports, California proved untenable because of its higher costs and because our design operations and manufacturing would still be thousands of miles away in Maryland. Closer to home, we began surveying the Baltimore–Washington corridor and found high volumes of unoccupied warehouse space, a testament to larger market trends of industrial consolidation and the flight of domestic manufacturing overseas.

We settled on a run-down, two-story, 125,000-square-foot warehouse in Glen Burnie, Maryland. Located near the Baltimore airport and shipping ports, it enabled us to receive raw materials easily by ocean or air. Best of all, it was inexpensive. This old, grungy space, built in the 1970s and occupied by a liquor distributor who had used it for storage, was far from the clean, well-organized, and professionally run warehouses dotting the region. But it was the least expensive facility on the market.

On my first visit, I roamed the giant facility, entirely vacant except for pallets of Johnnie Walker Black Label whisky. I tried to visualize how I would convert the storage space into a fully functioning factory. It lacked sprinkler and air conditioning systems, which would be indispensable for a candle factory, especially in Maryland's scorching summers. It had only two bathrooms, which was grossly inadequate to accommodate my hundred or so workers. The office space was too big, and I imagined putting some fresh paint on the walls and converting it into a photo gallery, where our PR and marketing teams could tell a visual story of our company, showcasing our previous Asian factories, pictures of our major collections, and photos taken with our collaborators from Target. I budgeted six to nine months to secure our permits, install sprinkler and air conditioning systems, and bring our space to code. If all went well, we would begin operations in June 2010.

Securing a permit was our first daunting task. Given the abundance of empty warehouses and the rhetoric of reshoring manufacturing, I thought my factory, which would make domestic products and employ Americans during a recession, might be welcomed. Instead, the government created every obstacle imaginable. Take the permit office in Glen Burnie's Anne Arundel County. Likely because Maryland hadn't seen a new factory since the 1990s, the office didn't have any codes for factories on the books. A government official presented us with thick booklets for hospitals, schools, and restaurants: "Be sure you meet all of these criteria and we'll give you a permit."

Meet all of the regulatory requirements for schools, hospitals, and restaurants—surely this man was joking. But he was entirely serious, and my mind began racing. We'd signed the lease on the warehouse and rental payments were soon due. Engineering and construction teams occupied the space, trying to make it code-ready. They constructed ramps next to the concrete stairs to comply with the Americans with Disabilities Act (ADA), installed more bathrooms, and hard-wired important safety systems. We'd also ordered expensive, state-of-the-art German candle-making machinery and assembly lines, along with shipments of glass, wax, and specialty fragrance supplies. If we didn't pass code, we'd have to store this expensive equipment at our own cost.

All government permitting took place over standard snail mail, ensuring that developments happened at a glacial pace. Every time we applied for a permit or our engineers submitted requests, it took over two weeks for the government office to receive our paperwork. At month-long intervals after initial receipt, we received several pages of improvements we needed to make. We'd scramble to fulfill those requests and comply with everything in the three books the permit office had given us.

David and I knew the American factory would be expensive. We'd budgeted $2.5 million to open our U.S. operation and 9 months to fulfill the permits. After 13 months, we'd spent $3.5 million.[1] Demoralized, I continued to navigate the nightmarish bureaucracy and watch my money disappear. Timothy Aeppel, a reporter who'd heard about a struggling new factory trying to open in the outskirts of Baltimore, contacted me one day: "We heard you are trying to open a manufacturing facility and getting no support. Is that right?"

I was vulnerable, and candidly shared my many business obstacles. The following day, May 5, 2011, the *Wall Street Journal*'s front cover story read: "Candle Maker Feels Burned." In detailing the regulatory problems I'd encountered in setting up my facility, there was a picture of me and my colleague Dale Williams, a home industry veteran and Chesapeake Bay's first chief operating officer who helped us navigate the factory's renovation. The two of us are pictured in the article looking over architectural plans with dour expressions on our faces.

Mei and her COO Dale Williams feeling discouraged about the American factory (2011).

The *Wall Street Journal* spread didn't ease my permitting troubles, but it did raise my national profile. Several years later, Congresswoman Judy Chu invited me to testify before the government's Committee on Small Business. A Democrat who'd represented California's 27th congressional district since 2009, Chu was the first Chinese American woman to occupy a congressional seat. When she asked me to speak about the state of manufacturing in America and the challenges of onshoring and reshoring, I was happy to do so.

On March 13, 2014, I testified at a congressional hearing alongside Shirley E. Mills, a Boston Company and Goldman Sachs alumna who specialized in American industry and utilities. We both argued that to maintain national competitiveness, our government needed to support small businesses looking to reshore. We suggested that federal and state governments sponsor a concierge program to help streamline regulatory hurdles and make the process more business friendly. After the testimony concluded, Chu and Mills needed to depart, leaving me with Tom Rice, the chairman of the committee and a conservative Republican representing South Carolina's 7th congressional district, and his colleagues. These congressmen and their aides, all Republican males, welcomed me to join them in a small restaurant near Capitol Hill. "No matter what we say," the congressmen said in unison, "nobody will listen to Republicans. They only care about Obama."

Sensing despair in their voices, and a frustration that their party would never again occupy the presidency, I was tempted to lend some perspective. After all, election victories are highly cyclical, with the major parties constantly rotating in and out of favor. But I didn't offer consolation because partisanship wasn't at issue here. Instead, we needed to broaden the discussion, I said that night, urging them to embrace thoughtful globalism, leverage manufacturing to power innovation and secure patents, and provide alternatives to education, so young people could take pride in learning trades instead of going into debt for expensive college degrees.

Made in Maryland

My worries didn't end after I managed to secure the necessary permits and begin production in June 2011. My first obstacle was managing a labor force unfamiliar with manufacturing. My first crop of factory workers comprised African American, Asian, and Latino Americans, as well as immigrants and Caucasian Americans who were mostly in their forties or fifties. They proved a great workforce who could operate forklifts and learn the assembly line, even if they lacked the ability to operate our advanced Germany machinery.

This capable workforce needed strong leaders and managers who understood the art and science of candle-making and could train our mixing specialists, arrange our factory lines—one for single-wick candles, another for multi-wick—and supervise the entire operational life cycle, from the placement of glasses from pallets to the cooling of candles prior to packaging. We needed factory visionaries who could imagine wax filling a tumbler and then schedule its movement around the factory floor so that it arrived at the end already semi-solid. Though I ultimately decided on the color and fragrance formulas, I needed laboratory specialists who understood math and chemistry and could proactively look for temperature irregularities in the machine monitors. I needed chemists who understood the way that pigments and dyes interacted with different concrete, glass, and ceramic vessels and how those in turn interfaced with any one of our 500-plus fragrances. Unlike my highly automated competitors who only needed a few factory workers to coordinate machines on the factory floor, I needed leaders who could train my 100 employees to work interdependently with the machinery.

Absent that visionary leadership, the first two years of American manufacturing were among the most stressful of my life. Though we'd been operating for 15 years, Chesapeake Bay felt like a startup, encountering the hardships that typically befall brand-new companies. As was the case during every recession, consumer demand for candles surged, as people wanted this affordable luxury to brighten their homes as well as the country's grim financial mood. Lacking strong managers, we couldn't train our labor force to meet this demand, resulting in lack of supply, quality deficiencies, and even more expenses.

During those two years, Richard and I hosted monthly management meetings that always handled bad news: broken glasses, misapplied labels, and bubbling wax from excess heat. On the supply side, we needed more raw materials to prepare for seasons like Falliday, and because of the new inventory-management requirements during the recession, we had to pay for storage. Each month David reviewed the financials, and with a look of dread on his face, said, "When are we going to stop the bleeding?"

I tried to muster my signature optimism, but even I felt hopeless. Instead of the healthy margins we'd experienced in Vietnam, we couldn't even cover the costs of American production. By 2011, we'd invested $6 million of our own cash into the business and morale reached new lows, especially among our young and bright office staff. When these sales teams received poor customer feedback because of quality problems, they despaired and initiated aggressive meetings with our product managers to identify problems in manufacturing.

Hope came from a January 2012 meeting I had at the White House. In late 2011, I received a call from the Boston Consulting Group asking if I'd join fellow CEOs to discuss reshoring and American manufacturing with President Obama, Vice President Biden, the White House Economic Council, and other related governmental agencies. I accepted. For my first trip to the White House, I donned a lavender suit and arrived at the executive building joining the CEOs of Rolls-Royce, Siemens' North America, DuPont, and Intel. As we filed around a long round table, I found my name at one end, and Ford Motor CEO Mark Field's on the other, with two blank seats separating us.

Barack Obama and Joe Biden entered the room and made the rounds, shaking everyone's hand. "What's up, Mei," Mr. Obama said, looking at my name card before sitting down to my right, with Joe Biden and Mark Fields seated next to him.

President Obama and Mei and the Insourcing American Job Forum (2012).

I wish I could say I did more to advance the cause of American manufacturing at that meeting. Instead, I remember becoming a little drowsy as everyone narrated their stories, and in desperate need of some coffee. Just when my caffeine cravings peaked, an aide entered the room and placed a cup of coffee next to the president. Obama is left-handed, meaning that the coffee was ideally positioned for my dominant right hand to snatch. My right hand instinctively extended forward, ready to grasp the coffee, before I retracted it, realizing it was meant for the president!

When the time came for me to share my story of jobs creation in America, Obama turned to me again and said, "So, Mei, what's your story?" Rather than telling him the story of the factory, I started telling him my life story, narrating my upbringing during China's Cultural

Revolution, attending boarding school to become a diplomat, and arriving in the United States expecting to see extraterrestrial life when I saw the sign "alien."

It suddenly dawned on me that I was grossly off-topic, and that the subject was business creation. Trying to quickly recover, I turned to Obama and asked, "Mr. President, what do you think our top-selling fall fragrance is?"

"Pumpkin," he replied. After mildly correcting him to "pumpkin spice," as I've narrated in a previous chapter, I shot him a smile and said, "It's all right, Mr. President, you can come and manage my factory."

He beamed at the well-meaning "candle lady" (a nickname I'm told he created for me).

Humor aside, I took my inclusion among corporate titans that day as a sign that top American leaders believed that even a small company like mine could bring jobs back to America. Before leaving the meeting, I shared this: "For other countries in the world, the label 'Made in America' means something. It stands for quality, consistency, and integrity. I'd like to see that label more."

It was my belief in that sentiment—a belief that I still have—that enabled me to endure the years of hemorrhaging money and persist with my dream of American manufacturing.

I'm glad I persevered because beginning around 2013, we reversed course and my Made in America gamble began paying off. Maryland was near some of the world's most innovative fragrance vendors scattered throughout the Atlantic seaboard, and I began compounding with more niche and boutique fragrance houses and facilities, allowing me to make small-batch orders for testing. Working with these small boutiques, instead of within far-flung supply chains with vendors requiring large orders, I could constantly adjust my formulas and exercise quality control. My close handling of these partnerships meant an end to copycat operations, and intellectual property and trade secret theft, all of which I suspected ran rampant in Asia.

The United States also provided us with more standardized raw materials like wax. I've described the challenges of working with Chinese-sourced petroleum wax, and the different mineral consistencies and product qualities that arrived at my factory from China's oil refineries. Over the years, I experimented with my wax formulas and even worked with non-petroleum alternatives like beeswax and soy. For consistency and performance, my principle candle ingredient had always been Chinese-sourced petroleum, which increased in cost each year, and which I shipped in big chunks, sometimes caked in mud and mineral deposits, to Vietnam. But when I began U.S. manufacturing, I sourced my wax and even some soy from Texas-based refineries, which arrived in liquid tanks. Working with my core ingredient already in liquid form proved advantageous. The American oil and gas industry, I soon discovered, observes rigorous refinement regulations that standardized my core ingredient and increased candle performances. Instead of detecting subtle gassy fragrance notes as I melted my wax, I could now more easily manipulate my fragrances, allowing my wax or wax-soy combinations to express subtle and elusive fragrance notes, like those required of my oxygen-based (or "ozonic") candles.

I could test the enhanced quality of American over Asian wax when performing my standard hot and cold throw procedures. Within the candle-making arts, "cold throw" refers to smelling a candle's scent when solid, while "hot throw" refers to performing the same test while the candle wax is illuminated. Customers routinely perform cold throws while browsing for candles in Target or in Bloomingdale's, and once they take their purchases home, they perform hot throws, evaluating the fragrance potency and quality while burning candles in their living areas or bathrooms. We applied a more scientific framework to these procedures in all of our factories, evaluating our fragrance strengths according to a 5-point grid. "From 1 to 5, how strong is the cold throw?" I might ask my first French-trained nose in the United States, Christelle Jardin.

Before moving to America, our cold and hot throws were in the 3 to 4 range, while after moving to Maryland, they consistently moved into the 5-point range. To achieve consistency, I tried to account for subjective biases that might influence throw evaluations. If you dislike a fragrance, for example, you'll likely rate it at an extreme because it stands out to you. If someone performing a throw test disliked lavender and rated it a 5, I discarded the result, along with extremes on the other end. We asked American focus groups to perform these tests, and once I accounted for extreme evaluations among all cohorts, consumers tended to converge with our factory readings, increasing my confidence in the results.

With these consistent source products, we were able to refine our brand's olfactory identity even further. Fragrance has always been the centerpiece of Chesapeake Bay's innovation, but after establishing our factory in the United States, I focused even more on scent, assembling an in-house fragrance committee of 10 to 12 people. Trying to keep my noses performing at their best, I invited fragrance vendors to test our team and see whose olfactive palette was keenest and sharpest. In addition to asking my committee to perform hot and cold throws, I evaluated their performances by asking them to identify the fragrance notes in unmarked sample scents. As a supertaster, I could sometimes smell hints of secondary notes like rose, eucalyptus, and mint. If I ever found someone who could identity the top three notes in a formula like me, or perhaps even more, I'd immediately recruit them to join the fragrance committee.

Ophélia Meldener could detect the subtlest of notes, and in 2011 I hired her as my fragrance manager, following Christelle Jardin in the mid-2000s. If Christelle helped us create a formidable fragrance-destination company, Ophélia appreciated my "fragrance first" vision for the brand, helping elevate us to the status of global innovator. While I had the genetic advantage of being a supertaster, Ophélia had the geographical advantage of having hailed from a small village outside of Grasse, France. Though she was a professionally trained nose, her homeland was probably her greatest teacher, nurturing her as it did in its endless acres of flowers that bloom all year long. At an early age, she learned to detect the rosemary, thyme, and basil seasons and distinguish them from the cypress, pine, and other woodsy scents that added complexity to these notes. She remembered the lavender blooms of early springs, the fig harvests in the warm summer months, and the beautiful mimosa flowerings in winter.

Ophélia's understated personality diverged from my outgoing nature, and her European sophistication and technical mastery contrasted with my eccentric creativity and unorthodox travel-based R&D. But together we were soul sisters of scent. If we were ever traveling together and forgot where we were, we played a little game, closing our eyes, and allowing the olfactory signature of the place to identify itself. The aromatic south of France contrasts with the gritty aroma of New York, and still again from Miami's moist, saline scent.

In addition to harnessing such creative talent, we invited our engineers and managers from the Vietnamese factory to assist us with process management and workflow. We gradually acquired technical mastery, learning the intricacies of our German machinery, how to service it, and when to rest it during peak season. We learned how to work the wicking machine and discovered one day that we'd been using defective glue to secure the wicks at the bottom of the candles for the first few years. As the back end improved, the front-end sales teams more routinely entered the factory, working alongside the design team to tailor their creations to the machinery. This had always been my dream: uniting all business units, especially manufacturing and design, to achieve the greatest heights in innovation and quality.

We experienced a breakthrough around 2013 with Target's Home Scent collection. This was the most innovative collection I'd made in Vietnam and one of the reasons for my onshoring in America. As I glanced at sales data, I saw dramatic volume increases. When manufacturing in Vietnam, I noticed that Target could sell 1,500 vanilla Home Scent jar candles each week. In 2013, Target sold up to 4,000 of the same candles, and this time they were "Made in the USA." We'd achieved greater quality and economies of scale, and consumers took notice. Consumers are extremely smart and savvy, and they could see and smell the different quality of American wax and fragrances, all the while enjoying the same affordable prices. Beginning in 2013, we used these increased volumes and quality to power not just innovation, but real growth. Finally, our design principles, sourcing, and marketing communications all reflected Chesapeake Bay's brand identity of quality, affordability, and proximity to nature.

With affirmation from Home Scent, my commitment to quality and passion for the manufacturing process blossomed. I loved watching glass vessels float around the factory floor, a sweet-smelling tide of cinnamon red or ocean blue dancing around the space before coming to a final destination in the assembly line, aligning like soldiers saluting a commanding officer. On the factory floor, I observed the chemical and physical reactions of the processes, noticing that when piping-hot liquid wax encountered cold glasses the vessels frosted, and how warming the glasses changed the texture ever so slightly. Subtleties like that proved key to our success. Chesapeake Bay was never as big as our competitors, but the sophistication of our finishes, like frosted or glossy glass, combined with the distinctive scents, made us unique.

While I had no problem ordering small runs and discarding entire batches or shipments because their cold throws rated only 3, I stopped doing that around 2013. Instead of suffering quality problems, my American-made collections proved higher quality than those I'd produced in both China and Vietnam. The quality was so impressive that every time I asked my big box chains like Target for price increases, my buyers usually granted them, as long as I ensured the same quality standards and delivery times.

Unlike in Vietnam, I now entered negotiations with leverage. Admittedly, the worst of the financial crisis was over. But consumers flocked to our high-quality Made in America products like never before. "Made in America" wasn't a marketing gimmick. My customers loved my products because their manufacture in America enabled high quality. And best of all, my American-powered innovation resulted in my greatest triumph in candle-making: the marriage of mind and body.

Taking Care of Mind and Body

Most of my major candle collections and ideas were born of freewheeling creativity, exotic travel, and joy. Inspiration arose during eccentric blue-sky design meetings on Friday afternoons in Maryland, while enjoying cocktails during R&D trips abroad, or at art shows, design expos, and beautifully curated boutiques. That wasn't true of "mind & body," my final candle collection and one of my proudest legacies to candle-making. This was a product of struggle and personal pain.

In 2015, I was stressed. David and I had finalized our divorce, and I spent every spare moment of my nonworking life crisscrossing Bethesda and downtown Washington, carting my two sons, Alex and Michael, to soccer games, birthday parties, and bar mitzvahs. I remember waking up bleary eyed on Saturday mornings, struggling to collect the right socks and equipment for a sports activity, and sometimes being so frazzled that I dropped the wrong boy off at the wrong competition. One exceedingly hot early summer afternoon in 2015, as I drove the boys down Bradley Boulevard's single and winding lane to Bethesda for the third soccer practice of the day, I nearly collided with another driver. She leaned heavily on her horn and flashed me a middle finger. As I collected myself at the side of the road, gently resting my head on the wheel, my mind turned to my calendar, full of endless meetings along with school events and recreational activities for the boys.

I'd taught my sons to work hard and exhibit generosity and goodness when dealing with others. But given my daily stress and chaos, and the anxiety and irritability that inevitably followed, I wasn't teaching them to attend to their own needs. I didn't prioritize my own wellness and self-care and I knew, after almost killing us all in a car crash, that it was for time for a change. My vision for "mind & body" began crystallizing that day.

Instead of just catering to others, I realized I needed to reconnect to my own emotional needs, inner self, and personal wellness. Instead of always fretting about the future, I needed to cultivate a relationship with the current moment. And perhaps I wasn't alone. Yoga, I reflected that day, was so popular throughout the world because it emphasized such personal reconnection. There was also a reason that Buddhist practices, like mindfulness and meditation, were then entering the global mainstream. Others probably found themselves just like me: slaves to their technological devices and jobs and longing to appreciate and savor the current moment. My new candle collection represented my personal journey and spiritual quest to connection—a quest I imagined that other stressed and frazzled people, especially women, might find compelling as well.

In this moment of personal pain and self-reflection, I spotted a powerful trend underway. Consumers sought wellness in their food products, shelling out massive amounts for locally sourced and organic products, even if it cost "whole paycheck" prices at Whole Foods grocery stores. Cosmetic companies joined in, launching clean beauty-product lines devoid of toxic ingredients and free of animal testing, while the automobile industry continued to pioneer electric and autonomous vehicles that didn't pollute the environment. These all formed part of the trillion-dollar wellness industry emphasizing purity in energy, food, beauty, and fashion. To contribute to this trend, I imagined an affordable candle collection that used soy wax and the highest-caliber essential oils to "fragrance" and "color" wellness-based emotions, improving health and human well-being.

The following week, I told my design team to prepare for a new mission: we would exit the realm of home fragrance and enter the wellness industry. To begin, we needed to delve deeper into the science of aromatherapy and color therapy, coordinating a range of emotions like harmony, peace, clarity, and balance with fragrances and colors. Uniting fragrance and color to evoke emotions like peace, balance, and self-care might strike observers as "fringe" or feel-good pseudoscience unless it had a solid scientific foundation.

My young and talented team listened to these ideas with excitement. My French nose, Ophélia, who understood the precise chemistry of scent, and my British designer, Denis Ryan, who understood graphic design with finesse, embraced the central idea informing the collection: "coloring" and "perfuming" the precise human emotions that evoked inner wellness. But it was still a challenge, especially given that aromatherapy and color therapy are two topics that remain underappreciated among scholars and the public at large.

Most of us intuitively understand the principles of color therapy. Just like fragrance affects our moods—cinnamon excites us, lavender relaxes us—color also exercises a profound effect on our psyches. Red is a vital color and represents love and passion in many global cultures. Blue, the color of the world's oceans and skies, universally signifies peace. The next time you are in a hospital, glance at the walls, and you'll likely see them coated in blue, helping to exert a calming influence on distressed people.

Color therapists have harnessed such deep color associations to address certain psychological challenges. In certain clinics, patients enter rooms entirely in dark blue, making them feel like they are living underwater and free; in other contexts, the rooms are entirely orange, making patients think of eating fruits and relaxing with friends. Some of these color associations are embedded from deep in our evolutionary history, while others change in step with societal norms. The popularity of millennial pink among men and women, for example, reveals that our society is becoming more gender neutral and that boys can like pink colors while girls can gravitate to conventionally masculine blacks and grays.

With my American factory, I now possessed the technical ability to attempt a combination of aroma and color therapies. Though I'd experimented with aromatherapy since launching a line called Spa in the mid-2000s, I lacked confidence in the quality of my source materials to launch a bona fide aromatherapy line from Asia. Now I could exercise the rigorous quality control over color and fragrance purity, harnessing the power of manufacturing to create just the right color, texture, and fragrance combinations to attempt such an imaginative line.

It took a full calendar year to generate a fragrance and color map to correspond to wellness-based emotions like peace, strength, and joy. Every Tuesday afternoon, my design team performed word-association exercises with me, matching emotions with fragrances and colors. Ophélia became skilled at this complex color/fragrance/emotion triangulation, and together with other members of our design team, we navigated some universal taboos and limitations about certain color associations.

Sandalwood, for example, can never be a bright green and must always accompany a neutral color like brownish gray. But light turquoise, we eventually determined, could represent harmony with nature and harmony with water. Blue alone was insufficient because it needed to combine with a life-affirming green to convey a sense of balance with the sun, moon, wind, and water. Turquoise reminded me of the coastal sandy waters in Mexico and the Caribbean and made me feel harmonious. (The larger Mediterranean and Atlantic oceans, by contrast, suggested more profound emotions, like passion and rage.) My biggest challenge remained tracing the effect of fragrance on emotions, and this turquoise proved no different. The team and I eventually matched it with water lily and pear, a botanical sweetness combined with ozonic notes.

That turquoise water lily pear candle anchored the entire collection. We then generated the second fragrance, settling on the beautiful and pure color of white, and the glorious emotions of peace and tranquility. Translating these emotions into fragrance proved difficult, but we veered toward jasmine in our meetings. On its voyage from Asia to the West, jasmine had become somewhat pigeonholed as a cool green. We created a cashmere jasmine scent to lend it a lighter feel and make it correspond to the warmth of tranquility and inner peace. From there, we generated confidence + freedom, my boldest design so far, comprising oak, moss, and amber, which celebrated my favorite fragrance category of all time: men's cologne (oriental fougere). This candle, rendered in beautiful French blue, was the wax equivalent of a fine luxury fragrance in a designer bottle.

To our surprise, purple proved a collection hit. We had three blues conveying reflection + clarity, confidence + freedom, and balance + harmony, so we needed a different color to express joy + laughter. Purple seemed ideal for this, and we fragranced it with fig and cashmere. As I've described, fig never works as a standalone fragrance for an American palette. But spiced fig was perfect. If you've ever nestled your nose into a fresh fig, you've noticed a beautiful scent—one that's more musky than fruity. Fig is warm without being overly feminine, and rather than communicate the fruit in a dry way, as its often found in stores, we spiced it up to match the red purple of its delightfully seedy fresh pulp. In the end, joy + laughter was a bright infusion of cassis (derived from black currants) and plum nectar, along with delicate rose and dahlia—a perfect balance between floral and fruity notes that couldn't help but produce a joyful accord.

To harness and express these fragrance-based emotions, we chose frosted finishes for our glasses. These semi-opaque vessels evoked the idea of creating and occupying a personal sanctuary, while the wooden lids communicated the warmth and authenticity found in nature. To make the collection as fresh and minimalist as possible, we decided against affixing labels on the glass, instead opting to silkscreen a dark gray script directly onto the surface.

We knew that this collection needed the perfect name. Just like Target's "Home Scents" or our popular "Heritage" collections, we needed something that our team, buyers, and consumers would recognize as the most mature expression of our brand story. We landed on the short and pithy "mind & body," rendered in lower-cased script to convey ease and minimalism.

With eight original fragrance/color/emotion combinations, this collection was simple and elegant as well as modern and thoughtful, making it accessible to everyone who sought to embark on or further their personal wellness journeys. We completed the collection with reed diffusers that could disseminate these fragrances without a flame. For the first time, I asked that our marketing department generate a visual brand to communicate the unique "mind & body" story. They conducted several photo shoots with models and from these photographs created a stylized black-and white figure of a woman seated in the lotus pose. With her back to the viewer and the phrase "mind & body" in black and white accompanying our signature logo, it was visually stunning, especially against our softly colored and frosted glasses.

As a wellness-oriented collection, applicable to everyone, I entered no exclusive agreements with any of my major retailers and focused on making the line universally available. To ensure fair competition, I insisted that prices be 100 percent uniform, so that mom-and-pop stores weren't at any disadvantage to Target.

When the first candles rolled off the assembly line in 2016, most were defective, and we briefly feared this would spell disaster. Technically, this represented the company's most ambitious fashion design yet, as we'd never attempted such density of words on such a diversity of frosted glasses. With 40 different colored glasses and size combinations, our quality was uneven, and we could only use 20 percent of this first order. We hadn't planned for these quality-control problems and hadn't given ourselves a buffer between production and shipment. We improvised by air-shipping some glasses to fill the first order.

Mercifully, we improved. The second shipment boasted a much higher percent acceptance, and by the end of the year, we moved from endcap to "inline," housing "mind & body" in a four-foot dedicated space within Target's candle valley. Within that first year, whatever stress we caused ourselves or Target was forgiven. We'd struck a consumer nerve and the collection hasn't stopped selling since.

"Mind & body" was my most successful candle collection, earning us great financial success and catapulting our brand recognition and popularity to new heights. The fragrance industry cited us as the first candle company to embrace the wellness trend. Comprising exercise, health foods, equipment, and so on, wellness was a $3.5 trillion a year industry, dwarfing the candle business's approximate $2 billion a year.[2] I detected the wellness trend early and used fragrance and wax to contribute to it. In 2014, when I began designing the line, Target decided that it wanted to compete against Walmart in the product categories of infant, design, and wellness. When asking Americans to shop those three categories, Target sought to outsell competitors like Walmart, and it succeeded. In fact, Target's focus around these three categories has allowed it not only to compete with Walmart, but also to thrive in the era of Amazon. Harnessing this wellness trend proved valuable for Target and for me—wellness was my most meaningful and popular trend-capture yet.

This collection helped power my factory's sales and increased retail distribution. The factory delivered outstanding products at surprisingly competitive prices, cultivated best practices, and enhanced innovation, all while improving quality. With the success of "mind & body," and its deep resonance on the market, my dreams of maximizing innovation and delivering luxuries at a reasonable price point were realized. The Maryland factory enabled the brand to reach its highest quality and fullest potential, and with this crowning achievement, the marriage of mind and body, we finally received the recognition I'd desired from consumers and retailers. I could retire happy and fulfilled.

Manufacturing the American Dream

In September 2011, Barack Obama delivered a speech to Congress extolling the benefits of domestic production:

> *If Americans can buy Kias and Hyundais, I want to see folks in South Korea driving Fords and Chevys and Chryslers. I want to see more products sold around the world stamped with the three proud words: "Made in America."*[3]

Obama's successor, Donald Trump, catapulted to office calling for a renaissance in American manufacturing, striking chords with an American electorate hungry for increased national self-reliance and more blue-collar domestic jobs. As much as it pleases me to hear such bipartisan support for American manufacturing, I've painfully experienced how such lofty rhetoric diverges from reality.

Part of the problem is cultural and educational. In countries like Japan, Germany, and Italy, all of which greatly esteem the "making of things," manufacturing has a higher social status than it does in the United States. Instead of exclusively pushing expensive four-year college degrees on young people, these countries offer internships and other hands-on learning opportunities that I craved here in America as I sought to learn about interior design and home fragrance, and that I wish I could have provided young people at my own factory.

America's corporate realm is also at fault. Leaders of large multinationals tend to focus on cost savings and competitiveness when considering manufacturing, treating it as a line item worthy of out-sourcing instead of a core business unit that drives innovation. As my experience shows, domestic production can be painfully expensive. But when corporate leaders take such a dim view of manufacturing, they're unable to leverage hands-on knowledge and design to solve problems and create new products and services, something I refer to as "design leadership."

Though I've routinely witnessed the prioritization of design and extraordinary design leaders in the first generation of major tech companies, I rarely see designers on boards of directors or occupying C-suite positions in the aerospace, energy, pharmaceutical, automo-tive, and semiconductor industries. As more visionary, design-forward company founders retire, classically trained managers take their place, all devaluing manufacturing and thereby stalling innovation.

It was only when I married design with manufacturing that I could achieve lasting and innovative product lines like "mind & body." After enduring financial pain and uncertainty, the opening of my American factory coincided with the most intensely design-focused, innova-tive, and profitable phase of Chesapeake Bay. Instead of creating an abstract idea and then sending it to be made overseas, I occupied a middle ground, creating ideas and then overseeing their physical real-ization on my factory floor. This not only eliminated corruption but also created efficiencies, as I learned where I could economize and where I needed to splurge to fine-tune my designs. When conceived as places of innovation instead of menial work, factories bridge the gap between imagination and execution, becoming centers of learning and knowledge. Simply put, they're where the magic happens.

- Have you ever faced an existential threat to your business? If so, change your business model or your manufacturing location, and instead of perishing you might just thrive. When manufacturing in China became impossible, Chesapeake Bay moved to Vietnam, where it leveraged a friendly and low-cost business climate to power a new wave of product innovation.
- Think carefully about outsourcing product manufacturing abroad. My American factory taught me that my creative potential could only be achieved—and transcended—with the marriage of innovation and manufacturing.
- Bringing manufacturing in-house, especially in America, might be expensive, but you'll decrease intellectual-property theft and other corruption, all the while increasing quality, powering innovation, and helping the environment.
- To maintain its national competitiveness, America must cultivate a new educational and business climate that encourages creative manufacturers as well as a culture that celebrates the "making of things" in general.

Endnotes

1. Timothy Aeppel, "Candle Maker Feels Burned," *Wall Street Journal*, updated May 5, 2011, https://www.wsj.com/articles/SB100014 24052748704463804576291594025772186.
2. These figures are approximate historical data. According to the Global Wellness Institute ("Wellness Industry Statistics & Facts, October 2018, accessed October 14, 2020, https://globalwellnessinstitute.org/ press-room/statistics-and-facts/#:~:text=The%20global%20 wellness%20economy%20is,%2C%20based%20on%20WHO%20data), the global wellness industry around 2018 was around a $4.5 trillion a year industry, while the American candle industry was $4.45 billion ("Industry Insights," *Grand Review Research*, accessed October 14, 2020, https://www.grandviewresearch.com/industry-analysis/ candles-market).
3. "Transcript: Obama's Speech to Congress on Jobs," *New York Times*, September 8, 2011, https://www.nytimes.com/2011/09/09/us/ politics/09text-obama-jobs-speech.html.

Conclusion

Sometime after I opened my American factory, a high-ranking politician from the US Department of Education visited the site to stage a job training event with local business leaders. As we walked the premises and met with workers, the politician casually said, "I don't want any plants making underwear to come back to America. Those shops can stay in China and Mexico."

As the founder of a consumer brand that had recently opened a US factory and created 100 American jobs, I couldn't help but wince. Candles are just like underwear, forming part of the undervalued, non-technology-driven manufacturing sector. As I've described in this book, such ideas have plagued my business journey, preventing venture capitalists from investing in my company when I began in China and causing me constant headaches with potential supply partners who grimaced at my small volumes and "inconsistent" snowflake textures. As I also detailed, anti-manufacturing prejudice followed me to the United States, where I learned that the country welcomes technology jobs but makes reshoring manufacturing for operations like mine extremely difficult.

On the factory floor that day, I also realized that this politician's comment crystallized America's central problems with entrepreneurship and manufacturing. When American companies began offshoring factory jobs in the 1970s, post–World War II prosperity declined. In the following decades, our understanding of innovation narrowed, as entrepreneurs increasingly gravitated to computer hardware and digital technology. In today's America, innovative technology companies, along with their high-paying tech jobs, reign supreme in the cultural imagination, while consumables like underwear are undervalued and outsourced.

When I consider how America might help create a new age of globalization that benefits all participants in the marketplace, my mind returns to underwear. What's wrong with manufacturing undergarments in the United States? When my sons were children and teenagers, their underwear fit badly and performed poorly during athletic events for the same reason that women's bras are uncomfortable: we're still largely using textile designs from the 1950s.

Instead of maximizing innovation in product categories like underwear, we've tried to minimize prices—to our collective detriment. As I've described in this book, my big-box retailers and candle-making competitors operated according to a "lowest price, highest margin" paradigm, creating an unprofitable, non-innovative, and wasteful retail ecosystem. Instead of using consumer needs and pain points to power innovation, retailers use discounts to spur consumer demand. Their margins have suffered as a result, and so have consumers who make do with poorly made products like itchy, unbreathable undergarments, waiting for discounts to purchase more. Our fixation on price instead of design-based innovation has damaged businesses, shareholders, consumers, and the planet.

The relentless pursuit of low prices in the clothing industry, for example, has given rise to fast fashion. Fast-fashion retailers like H&M are largely copycat operations that imitate high-end designers. Overproducing by about 50 percent, they flood their stores and e-commerce channels with quickly made, cheap merchandise, always keeping more than enough inventory on hand to capitalize on large-volume end-of-season sales. At the conclusion of these seasonal sales, they burn the remaining fashion items, resulting in air pollution, water pollution from toxic dyes, and unnecessary energy consumption.

Spotting a market opportunity, entrepreneurs have created ethical retail outlets, using transparent product sourcing, environmental stewardship, and design-driven fashions to attract customers. Instead of trying to compete with Banana Republic and J. Crew on product pricing, clothing companies like Everlane use sustainability and hyper-transparency as market advantages, systematically enumerating the material, labor, and shipping costs for every customer to consider when purchasing their elegant blouses and pants. Unlike large shoe brands that leverage celebrity endorsements and vast product lines to power growth, Allbirds shoe company uses design leadership to create eco-conscious product offerings. Like me, the founders of Allbirds let nature inspire their innovations, converting the plentiful amounts of New Zealand sheep hair into breathable, comfortable, and durable running shoes. Substituting marketing gimmicks for richly textured Merino wool, Allbirds consumes 60 percent less energy than their synthetic shoe-making counterparts, appealing to consumers interested in reducing pollution and helping the earth while also enjoying cool shoes.[1]

We can only create a more entrepreneurial and innovative economy if we have the courage to create and patronize companies like Everlane and Allbirds. Instead of fixating on price, these companies create design-driven products that benefit workers, consumers, suppliers, and the planet. I endeavored to do this at Chesapeake Bay, experimenting with different product designs and finishes, allowing design-based innovation instead of pricing to dictate my business decisions. My proudest achievement was my "mind & body" collection because it was on-trend and timeless, geared toward enhancing human wellness. It also proved to me that a medium-sized company, premised in design leadership, could prosper in America. With the success of my design-driven company, along with the growing visibility of ethical retail outlets like Everlane and Allbirds, I'm optimistic that we can create a better economy and world.

With consumer spending representing 70 percent of US GDP, the choice is ours: Will we support sustainable and transparent businesses, or simply visit Amazon and purchase the cheapest product we can find? Don't mistake my vision as insular or protectionist: I believe that supply chains will and should remain globalized. Even when I reshored manufacturing to America and began working with local, boutique vendors, I still sourced glasses from Asia and fragrances from Africa, South America, and Europe. Instead of championing the extremes of narrow protectionism or unrestrained global capitalism, I want American consumers to embrace a more thoughtful approach to product sourcing and purchasing, which might allow for us gradually to take more pride in design and the actual making of things and inspire us to support design-driven, sustainable businesses.

An economy premised on thoughtful consumerism and esteem for manufacturing is creative and inclusive. Operators in such an economy will naturally apply innovation to underwear, asking how we can create the most comfortable bras for women and breathable underwear for children, so that they feel their best all day. I still sometimes hear people say that, compared with China's rapid economic rise, America's best days are behind it. If we embrace a thoughtful economy, competing on quality instead of on price, that won't be the case. If entrepreneurs can look at unglamorous product categories—like candles and underwear—spotting moments to innovate, like I did at Bloomindale's in the 1990s, and launching new product lines, we'll remain nationally competitive for generations to come.

As a young girl in China, growing up in a sheltered society, I dreamed of many things. But I never could have imagined where life's journey would lead. From my early struggles to my seat at the table with President Obama, I have learned that grit, innovation, and a dash of luck are key to realizing the promise of America.

Endnote

1. Allbirds.com; Jacob Gallagher, "How the 'World's Most Comfortable Shoe' Is Challenging Nike and Adidas," *Wall Street Journal*, May 21, 2018, https://www.wsj.com/articles/how-the-worlds-most-comfortable-shoe-is-challenging-nike-and-adidas-1526917726.

About the Author

Mei Xu is a Chinese American entrepreneur and the founder and CEO of three global companies, Pacific Trade International, BlissLiving Home®, and Chesapeake Bay Candle®. Xu successfully negotiated the sale of Chesapeake Bay Candle to Newell Brands in 2017, a conglomerate with a $14 billion portfolio of consumer goods. Mei is now focused on helping women-owned consumer product companies grow and prosper with the *Yes She May* product platform (https://yesshemay.com/).

Born in Hangzhou, China, in 1967, Xu came of age during China's transformation to a more open, market-oriented economy following Chairman Mao Zedong's death in 1976. At age 12, Xu attended an elite language immersion boarding school designed to train diplomats for the foreign service.

Xu continued her education at Beijing Foreign Studies University, but her goal of entering the diplomatic corps was never realized, due to the 1989 Tiananmen Square uprising. At great personal and financial hardship, Xu moved to the United States to begin graduate school at the University of Maryland, College Park. After completing her master's degree, Xu moved to New York to work for a high-tech medical company that exported equipment to China. Unsatisfied with the meager salary and position, Mei and her then-husband, David, turned to entrepreneurship. Capitalizing on the beginnings of Sino-American relations, Xu began experimenting with making candles in her basement using Campbell's soup cans as molds. She then launched her consumer lifestyle brand. Her mottled and botanical-fragranced candles launched her brand to surprising success, and during her career she pivoted into the home fragrance and wellness industries.

After selling the company to Newell Brands, Mei created *Yes She May* to give women-owned brands a platform to reach a larger audience. It is the only online platform where consumers can shop for fashion, beauty, wellness, and home from women-owned businesses around the world. Each product is carefully curated so that no two brands compete in the same product space.

Xu's entrepreneurial success story has been reported on by major news organizations, including the *Wall Street Journal,* the *Washington Post,* NPR, the *Baltimore Sun,* CNBC, and MSNBC, among others.

Xu is an engaging storyteller whose personal journey to entrepreneurship inspires others. She is frequently invited to speak at universities, including the Wharton Business School, the Robert S. Smith School of Business at the University of Maryland, Georgetown University, Tsinghua University in Beijing; by business groups, including Fortune's Most Powerful Women and Horasis Global Visions Community; and government agencies, including the White House, where she was a panelist at the "Insourcing American Jobs" forum hosted by President Barack Obama. Xu's presentation topics and areas of expertise include women's global economic empowerment, entrepreneurship, made in America/reshoring initiatives, consumer lifestyle trends, the importance of a global education, and business development in China. Xu has also shared her story of entrepreneurial success with the host of the TED Radio Hour and "How I Built This with Guy Raz" on NPR.

Xu's business achievements have repeatedly been recognized by prominent organizations. She has received, among others, the Brava Award from Smart CEO; the Maryland International Business Leadership Award from the World Trade Center Institute; the Business Leader of the Year Award from the Asian American Chamber of Commerce; the Entrepreneurial Leadership Award from the Asian Women in Business Organization; the Women Who Mean Business Award from the *Washington Business Journal*; the Most Admired CEO Award from the *Maryland Daily Record*; and the Philip Merrill College of Journalism Distinguished Alumnus Award from the University of Maryland. Xu was also inducted into the Enterprising Women Hall of Fame and named twice by *Inc.* magazine as CEO of one of America's Fastest Growing Privately Held Companies.

Xu plays and active role in community, philanthropic, and civic organizations, serving on boards of both for-profit and nonprofit organizations, including Sandy Spring BanCorp, Inc. (2012–2015); the University of Maryland, Baltimore Foundation; World Affairs Council. She served as Chair of the Meridian International and is serving on many investment boards including Halcyon Incubator Fund in Washington D.C. which support social entrepreneurship. In 2020 she created the Yes She May Entrepreneur Grant to award winners of Annual Business Pitch by the female students at Bowie State University in Maryland, a mostly African American University, to help bring equality and opportunity to African American female business. Xu is also a member of the Committee of 200(C200), and invitation-only organization of the world's most successful women entrepreneurs and corporate innovators; the Aspen Institute's Society of Fellows; and member of US-China Business Council. She is a delegate to Fortune's Most Powerful Women Summit; a mentor with the Fortune/U.S. State Department Global Women's Mentoring Partnership; and a WE Connect Founding International Ambassador.

Xu and her family live in Bethesda, Maryland. To contact Mei, please visit: info@meixu.com.

Mei Xu

Founder & CEO

YesSheMay.com

Acknowledgments

After I stepped down as CEO of Chesapeake Bay Company in November 2018, people began asking me how I built my business. How did I think of it? How did I operate it across several continents? How did I navigate ever-changing consumer trends? My then-publicist Sherri Cunningham and my literary agents Robin Sproul, Dylan Colligan, and Keith Urbahn somehow convinced me that my journey as a businesswoman and immigrant could shed light on questions of entrepreneurship, innovation, manufacturing, and American national competitiveness. They helped me convert and shape my journey into book form.

And then there was writing the book. As we sheltered in place during the COVID-19 pandemic, I leaned into the research and writing with my collaborator and writing partner, Rachel Gostenhofer. When we first embarked on this project, the two of us planned to traverse Asia, journeying to my hometown and visiting my factories in China and Vietnam. The pandemic placed an extra burden on our research and imagination. With our different aesthetics and points of view, we tried on different voices and experimented with different stories, ensuring that we achieved cultural, historical, and emotional truth. I also want to thank my fellow writing collaborator, Seth Shulman. His critical feedback and strategic insight were as indispensable as his clarity and precision.

As I labored away on the writing, my expert and wonderful editorial team at Wiley—Jeanenne Ray, Dawn Kilgore, Gary Schwartz, and Sally Baker—gave me significant confidence and rooted me at each stage of the process. I am especially grateful for the creative license that they provided me to lead the writing and story arc in the way I deemed fit.

My sincere gratitude goes to my sister, Li Xu. Early on, she took a major risk—leaving a comfortable and stable career to join my hair-brained scheme of creating scented candles and home fashion accessories. She's been by my side from the glow-candle days and was indispensable as the company scaled and took exciting new turns, like opening a factory in America. Many thanks are also due to Michael Sheng, who succeeded Li as CEO of the factory and the Asian operation and continues to find new opportunities to grow the company.

Richard Zhu, my long-term business partner and friend who also retired with me in 2018, was indispensable in operating Chesapeake Bay Candle, as was his help with the details mentioned in this book. Many thanks to David Sunberg for his steadfast work in helping me with the Target account, as well as for his help in remembering important details and stories captured in this book.

My nose, Ophélia Meldener, and my senior designer, Corina Heymann, also provided extensive interviews, making this story more accurate and vivid. They were two of my creative pillars at Chesapeake Bay, journeying the world with me to capture trends and, once home, devising innovative scents and product-packaging solutions. I'm so pleased that we could collaborate again creatively in the form of this book.

Additional thanks go to the many people who helped me establish the company, including Sharon Sittig, Carmen Au, Elaine Bauer, Carmen DeSenne, David Lonis, Karl Martin, Mareike Finck, Dale Williams, Jennifer Turner, Jorge Filippi, Rachel Villareal, Renee Drumgold, Charene Stewart, Kristen Anderson, Ruth Considine, Quynh Le, Smith Zheng, Joe Barros, Cesar Carbajal, Denis Ryan, Elliott Dean, Emily Eisenstadt, Ghatsinne Ann Salcedo, Gira Parikh, Gwyeneth Stamegna, Jacqueline Coronado, Jenna Fanning, Jennifer Bassinger, Jennifer Rizzo, Kimberly Nguyen, Kristen Rinelli, Kristin Anderson, Maria Jarvis, Mariecel Monroyo, Molly Rodriguez, Paul Renner, Lawrence Law, Stacy Ohana, Lindsay Brown, Luisa Maldonado, Lynn Maher, Laura Carter, Piumi Perera, and Samantha Raum.

Among the people who supported me in my journey at Chesapeake Bay and beyond, I especially want to thank my executive assistant extraordinaire, Maria Mesina. She was particularly helpful during moments of personal challenge and major transitions, like when I stepped down as CEO and during the year-long process of writing this book.

And last, but certainly not least, I want to thank my talented, loving, and handsome husband, Alessandro Rebucci. He brings a watchful economist's eye to everything we do together—including this book—always encouraging me to "stick to the facts." Though he's not featured in this book, he's my true North Star, guiding my journey through life. Physically and metaphorically, he is a towering presence in my life.

And finally, to my children. Alex and Michael arrived in my life just when Chesapeake Bay became a truly design-driven company. They enabled me to become my most creative and productive self, thanks to the joy and happiness they've continually brought to my life. They remain my greatest accomplishments in this world. My stepchildren, Lara and Lucas, have also provided love and support, continually reminding me of how cross-cultural exchange increases the richness of our lives. As second-generation immigrants, I hope that all four of our children never lose their pioneering spirit and sense of curiosity, wonder, and hunger that accompanies so many of us who journey to distant lands in search of a better life.

—Mei Xu

Index

A

Aeppel, Timothy, 128
Alcohol-based fragrance formulas, experimentation, 112
Alibaba, founding, 62
Allbirds, design leadership (usage), 146–147
Alzheimer's disease (AD), treatment (objective), 12, 116–118
Ambers, compounding, 101
Ambiente trade show, 48, 59, 95, 96
  candles, (reevaluation), 49–50
America Dream, 42, 54, 142
Americans with Disabilities Act (ADA), 128
Antidumping tariffs, impact, 120
Anti-merchant prejudices, 62–64
Aphrodite, fragrant offering, 102
Aroma Bay Candle (Vietnam factory), 121
Aromatherapy, powers, 115, 139

B

Bed Bath & Beyond
  deal, 70–73, 77, 121, 123
  orders, problems, 89
  pitch, 75
  replenishment vendor status, 72
Beeswax, usage, 133–134
Beijing
  college, Xu arrival, 22

  university district, student perception, 28
Beijing Foreign Studies University, Xu interview, 21
Beijing University, ideas/progress, 28–29
Biden, Joe, 131–132
Bleeding (wax), 67
Bloomingdale's, 109
  cross-merchandising, impact, 69
  deal, 68–69
  orders, problems, 89
  pitch, 75
  Xu visit, 42–43
Body language, reading, 46–47
Boston Consulting Group, 131
Box stores, vendor entry (difficulty), 70
Brand
  identity, change, 59–60
  sensory branding, 106
  transformation, 110
  visual brand, generation, 141
Briefcase guy, 44
Buildings
  building-based fragrance stories, awareness, 106
  fragrance stories, 105
Burn
  behavior, 66
  non-draft burn tests, performing, 66
  times, inconsistency, 67

C

Calligraphy styles, 60
"Candle Maker Feels Burned" *(The Wall Street Journal),* 128–129
Candles
  Ambiente trade show, 49–50, 59
  analyses (Heymann), 94–95
  assembly line (Vietnam) (photo), 122
  bottom, wick (insertion), 66–67
  brand identity, change, 59–60
  burn behavior, influences, 66
  candle-making
    elements, creative possibilities, 95
    maturation, 73
  Chicago Gift Show success, 47–48
  classic collection, 97–98
  colors/fragrances, 52
    palette/vision, alignment, 52–53
  consistency, requirement, 61
  cross-merchandising, 69
  design-based innovation, 53–54
    importance, 50
  finishes, 96
  frosted appearance, 96
  glass vessels, usage, 110
  glow candles
    business, 63
    popularity, 45–46
  jar candles, popularity, 125–126
  Kirkland's orders, 47
  life/longevity, answers, 46
  linen finish, production, 96
  magic glow candles, manufacture, 63
  New York International Gift Fair sales, reevaluation, 48–49
  non-draft burn tests, 66
  nonflammable home-fragrance products, pursuit, 110–111
  nonuniformity/uniqueness, problems, 70
  oxygen-based (ozonic) candles, 134
  popularity, 45–46
  product
    design, improvement, 48–49
    quality, ensuring, 64–65, 90, 123
    regional quality, variation, 65–66
    reorders, speed, 47
    stand-alone pillars, usage, 110
    Vybar, usage (absence), 53
    white vanilla candle, creation, 66
    YInMn Blue, patent, 87
Canton, haute cuisine capital, 10–11
Chanel Nº5, 100, 111
Chargeback, receiving (potential), 79
Chesapeake Bay (company)
  antidumping tariffs, impact, 120
  anti-merchant prejudices, 62–63
  Bed Bath & Beyond deal, 70–71
  Bloomingdale's deal, 68–69
  box candles, Target launch, 124
  brand, transformation, 110
  buyers, advance 12-month cycle, 71
  candles, air-shipping, 85–86
  capital, search, 63–64
  Chinese candle manufacturer, partnership, 61
  classic collection, 97–98
  collaborators, 63–64
  color/olfactory mixture, 66–67
  company, creation, 59
  competition, 86, 125
  Copper Moon (fragrance), 109
  design
    focus, 91
    process, travel (impact/increase), 96–97
    studios, opening, 95
    team, research, 97
  design-focused company, transformation, 95
  design-forward brand, Chinese counterparts (divergence), 60
  failure, learning, 67
  Friday blue sky trend meetings, 98
  Full Moon (fragrance), 109
  Glen Burnie warehouse (Maryland), manufacturing move, 127–131

goodwill, leveraging, 125
Great Recession, impact, 124–125
growth, 70
high-interest lending, usage, 64
"Home Scents" collection, 123, 125
humidifier, creation, 113
inspiration library, 97
"Jasmine Water" (scent), 103
labor costs, increase, 124–125
lead cap allotment (Target), 77–78
Lemongrass Eucalyptus (fragrance), 103
magic glow candles, manufacture, 63
manufacturing locations, alternatives, 120–121
marketing, 67–68
Mediterranean Citrus (fragrance), 103–104
Nordstrom deal, 70
Oak Moss Amber (fragrance), 103–104
operational complexity, fears, 61
osmanthus, creation, 104
overseas production, increase, 80
personal savings, usage, 64
pillar candles (photo), 54
Portu Sunberg, partnership, 84–85
process management/workflow, assistance, 135–136
product
  consistency, difficulty, 64–65
  cross-merchandising, 69
  nonuniformity/uniqueness, problems, 70
  quality, ensuring, 64–65, 90, 123
production
  establishment, 64
  increase, 84
profitability, increase, 84
redistribution window, reduction, 82
regional quality, variation, 65–66
replenishment vendor status, 72, 89
revenue projections, problems, 85–86

sales, projections, 86
sell-throughs (complications), promotions (impact), 71–72
shipment delay, 81–82, 87
small-batch orders, 133
"Sonoma" jar-candle line, 123
Spa line, 139
spring, retail season (importance), 71
standard operating procedures, updating, 67
tchotchke reputation, avoidance, 60
Temple (fragrance offering), 102
travel, usage, 96–97
vendor size, transformation, 84
warehouse rental, 81–82
wellness industry entry, 138–139
Chesapeake Bay (location)
  olfactory identity, 108
  peace, 58
Chesapeake Bay/Target
  collaboration, importance, 90
  deal, 77–80
  dissimulation, problems, 88
  first order, 81–84
  partnership
    salvaging, 85–86
    survival/lessons, 86–87
  pitch, 75–77
  research/contact, 72–75
  sales, projection, 86
  shipment delay, 87–88
Chicago Gift Show, candles (sales success), 47–48
China
  bureaucracy, Xu navigation, 34–36
  control, consolidation, 7
  isolationism/internationalism, change, 16
  Japan invasion (1937), 6
  marketplace success, 62
  Open Door policy, 16
  self-expression, ideological opposition, 60
Chu, Judy, 129

Cleopatra, fragrances (usage), 101
Clinique, Happy (debut), 108
Cold throw, 134–136
Cold War, 7, 121
Color therapy, 139
  purple, popularity, 140
Communist Party, food
    (rationing), 10
Consumer response, supply-chain
    management system response
    (Target), 79
Copper Moon (fragrance), 109
COVID-19 pandemic, impact, 120
Cross-merchandising, 69
Cultural Revolution (China), 2, 6, 28,
    39, 51, 132–133
Customer
  behavior projections,
      understanding, 79
  complaints, imagining, 83
  demand, increase, 84

D

Dalian, 29–30, 34–36, 40–41
Dapoly, 51
Democratization of design
    philosophy, 73–74
Desenne, Carmen, 99–101
Design leadership, usage, 146–147
Design/manufacturing combination,
    impact, 143–144
Diffusers
  delivery, 112
  reed diffusers, 111–113

E

Emotions
  emotional response system,
      fragrances (impact), 114
  fragrance-based emotions, control/
      expression, 140–141
End-of-season markdowns, 80
English Corners, emergence, 27
Enlai, Zhou

China consolidation, 7
Enlai, Zhou (grandparent figure), 6–7
Entrepreneurship, American
    perception, 145–146
Environmental factors,
    impact, 115–116
Everlane, sustainability/
    hypertransparency, 146–147

F

Falliday season, 47, 71–72
  discussion, 82
  fragrance stories, 103
  stress, 74
Fancy Food Show, visit, 94
Fashion, global cultural
    expression, 43
Fashion Week, 105
Fields, Mark, 132
First Five-Year Plan (Zedong), 62
Food, indulgence (safety), 14
Fragrance
  alcohol-based fragrance formulas,
      experimentation, 112
  cocktail-inspired fragrances,
      conception, 98
  delivery, 109–114
    innovation, challenge, 111–113
  effects, 114–115
  failures, 107–108
  fragrance-based emotions, control/
      expression, 140–141
  graph, usage, 114–115
  home fragrance, Chesapeake
      Bay exit, 138
  houses, contact (increase/
      importance), 101
  industry, start, 52
  infusions, usage (Chinese
      doubts), 61
  instructor, hiring, 52–53
  journey, 99–101
  layering, 111
  legacy, 114–117

natural fragrance-delivery systems, creation, 113
notes, aspiration, 108–109
science, 108–109
signature scents, manufacture/ diffusion, 105
story failures, 106–107
storytelling, 101–109
"Fragrance first" vision, 135
Fragrance Foundation, invitation, 99–101
French Color & Fragrance Co., 52
French, Peter, 52, 61, 114
Friday blue sky trend meetings, 98
Full Moon (fragrance), 109

G

Gaokao (National College Entrance Examination), 20–21
Glen Burnie warehouse (Maryland)
  bureaucracy, navigation, 128–129
  manufacturing move, 127–131
  quality, 136–137
  workforce, assembly, 130–131
Glow candles. *See* Candles
Gorbachev, Mikhail, 29
Grasse ("Rome of scents"), 100, 135
Grasses, preparation, 112
Graves, Michael, 73–74
Gray goods, circulation, 13
Great Depression, 42
Great Proletarian Cultural Revolution, focus, 11
Great Recession, 120
  impact, 124–125

H

Hangzhou
  entrepreneurial mecca, growth, 62
  harmony, 9–15
  iron/steel mill, 9
  middle school, entry exam, 15–22
  scenic appeal, 4
  three flowers, 22, 27

urban development, vestiges, 3–4
visit (1996), 61
West Lake district, 58, 104
Xu, birth, 3
Hangzhou manufacturing facility
  failure, learning, 67
  photo, 65
  securing, 64
  standard operating procedures, updating, 67
Happy (Clinique debut), 108
Heilongjiang (reeducation camp), 8
"Heritage" collection, 141
Heymann, Corina, 94, 98
  candle analyses, 94–95
Hirsch, Alan R., 116
Holiday season orders, discussion, 82
Home interiors
  revolution, 43
  Xu/David research, 44
Home Scent collection ("Made in the USA"), 136
"Home Scents" collection, 123, 125, 141
Hong Kong, market experimentation, 28
Hot throw, 134
House of Chanel, rose source/ compounds, 100
Human emotions, coloring/ perfuming, 139
Human wellness (promotion), fragrances (impact), 114
Humidifier, creation, 113

I

Innovation, maximization (goal), 146
Inspiration library, 97
Intellectuals, perspective, 10
International Flavors & Fragrances (IFF), Xu journey, 114
Inventory databases, retailer tracking, 71

J

Jardin, Christelle, 134–135
Jars
  jar candles, popularity, 125–126
  usage, 110
  vessels, experimentation, 122–123
"Jasmine Water" (scent), 103
Jo Malone
  handmade candles/boxes,
      sourcing, 123–124
  visit/research, 123
Just-because bouquets, oil yields, 101

K

Kai Shu (Chinese standard script), 60
Kalbermatten, John/Nelly
    (Xu visit), 37–39
Kirkland's, candles orders, 47
Kohl's, "Sonoma" jar-candle line, 123
Kors, Michael, 80

L

Labor costs, increase, 124–126
Langer, Ellen, 115–116
Laurel (Maryland), office space
    rental, 44–45
Lead cap, allotment (Target),
    77–78
Lean product-supply model
    (Target), 79
Le Labo, Santal 26 creation, 105
Lemongrass Eucalyptus
    (fragrance), 103
Li, meaning, 14
"Linger-longer factor," 106
Lingyin Temple, scent
    (association), 102

M

Magic glow candles. *See* Candles
Maison & Objet trade show
    (Paris), 97, 106
Ma, Jack, 62

Manufacturing, American
    perception, 145–146
Market opportunity, entrepreneur
    identification, 146
Market socialism, China
    (approach), 16
Meditation, 138
Mediterranean Citrus
    (fragrance), 103–104
Mei-isms, 89–90
Mei, meaning, 14
Mei's Pod, 113–114
Meldener, Ophélia, 135, 138–139
Middle school, Xu attendance, 15–22
Mills, Shirley E., 129
"Mind & body"
  collection, success, 142–143
  story, communication, 141
Mindfulness, 138
Monique, Queen, 2
Mood boards, creation, 95
Moods, fragrances (impact), 139
Musk, compounding, 101

N

Nagel, Christine, 109
National College Entrance
    Examination. *See Gaokao*
New Oriental Education &
    Technology Group Inc., service
    (initiation), 28
New York City, Xu (arrival), 39
New York International Gift Fair,
    candle sales (reevaluation), 48–49
New York Times, The (Xu reading), 39
Niche markets, Xu/David
    search, 43–44
Nixon, Richard (PRC visit), 16
Non-draft burn tests performing, 66
Nordstrom
  deal, 70
  pitch, 75
Noses, 100
  interactions, 108

O

Oak Moss Amber
     (fragrance), 103–104
Obama, Barack, 9, 11, 102, 131–133,
     142–143, 148, 150
  Xu/Obama photo, 132
Obama, Michelle (Mei designed
     candle), 107
Ocular overload, 116
Oils
  oozing, 67
  rose oil production,
       difficulty, 100–101
  wax/colors, blending, 53
  wax/dyes, interaction, 66
  yields, 101
Olfactory experiments, objective, 117
Olfactory identity, 108
One World Trade Center, signature
     scent (creation), 106
Open Door policy (China), 16
Osmanthus, creation, 104
Overcommunication, importance, 88
Oxygen-based (ozonic) candles, 134

P

Pacific Trade International
  formation, 44
  growth, 50
  products (photo), 45
  reorders, speed, 47
  representatives, hiring, 50–51
  social/business setting, David
       (success), 46–47
People's Republic of China (PRC)
  creation, 6
  Nixon visit, 16
Perfume houses, interaction, 108
Perfume: The Story of a Murderer
     (Süskind), 98
Petroleum was (paraffin wax), usage,
     64–65, 109, 112, 133–134
Planogram, 83

creation, 78
  walkthrough, problems, 85
Pol Pot (Khmer Rouge
     dictatorship), 2
Portu Sunberg, Chesapeake Bay
     partnership, 84–86
Prices, minimization (problems), 146
Product
  innovation, focus, 95
  manufacturing locations,
       alternatives, 120–121
  nonflammable home-fragrance
       products, pursuit, 110–111
  quality, ensuring, 64–65, 90
Pumpkin spice, fragrance stories,
     102–103, 133

Q

Quality, ensuring, 64–65, 90, 123

R

Reed diffusers, 111–112, 123
  introduction, 112–113, 141
Reichenback, Carl, 65
Replenishment vendors,
     offerings, 72
Replenishment vendor status
  Bed Bath & Beyond, 72
  Target, 89
Retailers
  inventory databases, retailer
       tracking, 71
  post-holiday retail slump,
       ending, 71
Revolution, peril/promise, 6–9
Rice, Tom, 129
Rose oil production,
     difficulty, 100–101
Ryan, Denis, 138–139

S

Sales, improvement method, 94
Santal 26, fragrance (usage), 105

Schock, Jennifer, 74
  delivery request, 77
  photo, 80
  trouble (message), 83–84
  Xu meeting, 75–77
Self-expression, ideological
    opposition (China), 60
Sell-throughs, 71
  complications, promotions
    (impact), 71–72
  reports, 80
Sensory branding, 106
Shot glasses collection, creation, 98
Signature scents, manufacture/
    diffusion, 105
Sihanouk, Norodom, 2
Soy, usage, 133–134
Spa (Chesapeake Bay line), 139
Spring, retail season (importance), 71
Stand-alone pillars, usage, 110
Sunberg, David, 85, 105
  photo, 90, 105
Supply-chain disruptions, 79
Süskind, Patrick, 98–99

T

Target
  box candles, launch, 124
  buyers, team (photo), 80
  collaboration, importance, 90
  customer demand, increase, 84
  deal, 77–80
  design/quality differentiation,
    focus, 78
  dissimulation, problems, 88
  first order, 81–84
  Graves, impact, 73–74
  "Heritage" collection, 141
  Home Scent collection
    ("Made in the USA"), 136
  "Home Scents" collection,
    123, 125, 141
  lead cap allotment, 77–78
  lean product-supply model, 79

  merchandise, unloading, 83
  "mind & body" collection,
    success, 142
  operational challenges, 78
  overcommunication, importance, 88
  partnership
    salvaging, 85–86
    survival/lessons, 86–87
  pitch, 75–77
  planogram, creation, 78
  profitability, increase, 84
  racetrack layout, 72–73
  research/contact, 72–75
  sell-through reports, 80
  shipment delay, 87–88
  stock, depletion, 83–84
  vendor
    size, transformation, 84
    trainings, 79
  visual merchandizers,
    interaction, 78
Temple (fragrance offering), 102
Texture-forward glass vessels, 110
Trends, examination, 96–97
Trump, Donald (rhetoric), 143
Typhoon Babs, impact, 87

U

Undesirables, reeducation
    program, 8
United Nations Development
    Programme (UNDP), Xu
    (association), 23–25
United States, Xu arrival, 34
University of Maryland (College
    Park), Xu admission, 36–37
US-China Industrial Exchange (New
    York), Xu (job dissatisfaction/
    exit), 39–41, 44

V

Vendor trainings (Target), 79
Venture space, anti-merchant
    prejudices, 63–64

Vietnam
  antidumping costs, zero level, 126
  candles, assembly line (photo), 122
  fashion-driven jar-candle business,
    popularity, 123
  manufacturing location, 121
Vybar, usage (absence), 53

W

Wall Street Journal, The
    (Xu reading), 39
Walsh, Sharon, 51
Wang, David (photo), 80
Washington Post, The (Xu reading), 39
Washington (DC), Xu arrival, 37
Water-based diffuser, 106
Wax
  bleeding, 67
  cold throw, 134, 136
  consistency, achievement,
    134–135
  cooling, interruption, 96
  hot throw, 134
  innovation, continuation,
    110–111
  oils/colors, blending, 53
  oils/dyes, interaction, 66
  receptacles, usage, 53
  stones, melting, 66–67
Well-being (promotion), fragrances
    (impact), 114
Wellness
  candles, production, 141–142
  consumer search, 138
  industry, Chesapeake Bay
    entry, 138–139
White vanilla candle, creation, 66
Wholesale-focused trade shows,
    calendar (understanding), 44
Williams, Dale, 128
  photo, 129
World Bank
  China, debt, 25
  Xu, work, 23–25, 27, 29

X

Xiaomin, Shang, 19
Xiaoping, Deng, 2
  control, 16
  economic liberalization agenda, 62
Xu family (photo), 5
Xu, Li, 14
  business partnership, 62
  candle batch shipment, 68
  manufacturing facility, updating, 63
  photos, 5, 80, 104
  talent/studies, 14–15
Xu, Mei
  Beijing, collegiate language
    training, 22
  Beijing Foreign Studies University
    interview, 21
  Bloomingdale's visit, 42–43
  boarding school years, 13–20
  cultural horizons, expansion, 19–20
  cultural reflex, 88
  culture shock, 37–38
  David/Mei (photo), 26
  David, support, 41
  designer in chief, role/impact, 96
  design team (photo), 68
  divorce, 137
  father, job (demand), 12
  Glen Burnie photo, 129
  growth mindset, 89
  hunger, 17–18
  husband, meeting, 25–27
  hyper-transparency, approach, 90
  IFF visit, 114
  journalism degree, graduation
    (1992), 39
  language, learning, 17
  management meetings, 131
  margin assessment/financial
    projections, delivery, 89
  middle school entry, 15–22
  mother, military training/educator
    (role/impact), 10–12

Xu, Mei (*Continued*)
move (Dalian), 29–30
needs/self/wellness,
reconnection, 138
overcommunication, importance, 88
parents, roles (demand), 10
passport
granting, loophole/
bureaucracy, 34–36
obtaining, tuition repayment
(requirement), 30–31
photos, 3, 5, 80, 104, 105
poise/confidence, increase, 90–91
products, debut (photo), 45
retirement, 104
Schock meeting, 75–77
social contact, importance, 42
transparency/honesty, shift,
88–89
United Nations Development
Programme, association/
mission, 23–25
United States, arrival, 34
University of Maryland (College
Park) admission, 36–37

US-China Industrial Exchange
(New York), job (quitting), 44
US-China Industrial Exchange (New
York), job dissatisfaction, 39–41
Washington (DC)
arrival, 37
visit (Kalbermatten family), 37–39
World Bank, work, 23–25, 27, 29
Xu/Obama photo, 132

Y

Yaobang, Hu (death), 29
YInMn Blue, patent, 87

Z

Zedong, Mao, 60
death, 16
First Five-Year Plan, 62
reeducation program, 8
victory, 6
Zhu, Richard, 51–52, 89–90, 126
management meetings, 131
photo, 51
Zodax, competition, 111–112